A BLANDFORD GARDENIN

C000029151

Garden Planning & Design

Peter McHoy

BLANDFORD PRESS
POOLE · DORSET

First published in the U.K. 1984 by Blandford Press,
Link House, West Street, Poole, Dorset, BH15 1LL.

Distributed in the United States by
Streling Publishing Co., Inc.,
2 Park Avenue, New York, N.Y. 10016.

British Library Cataloguing in Publication Data

McHoy, Peter
 Garden planning and design.—(A Blandford gardening
 handbook)
 1. Gardening
 I. Title
 712'.6   SB450.97

ISBN 0 7137 1246 5 (Hardback)
      0 7137 1417 4 (Paperback)

Typeset in Hong Kong by Graphicraft Typesetters
Printed in Great Britain by A. Wheaton & Co., Ltd., Exeter

Contents

Acknowledgements

This is primarily a book about ideas — designs and devices that other gardeners have found to work. Wherever possible the author has illustrated the points with photographs of real gardens, most of them created by enthusiastic amateurs. He wishes to thank the many individuals whose gardens he has been able to photograph, and whose ideas we hope will inspire others.

The author would like to thank the following garden owners or designers (their gardens are illustrated on the pages in brackets): Miss Bell (122r); D. Earl Bicknell (106r, 108tl, 124r); Mr & Mrs R. Cameron (Great Comp) (116tl, 118l); Mr & Mrs L. Cliffe (10, 96t); Miss N. Clinch (19); Donald Farthing (Daily Express Garden, Chelsea Show 1982) (54); Mr & Mrs Fielding (15b, 95, 96b, 107tl, 122l, 125r); Mr & Mrs Graham Furguson (110br); Mr & Mrs Martin Furniss (Cobblers) (108tr, 121l, 121r); Barry Gray (97); Geoff Hudson (7, 102r, 103l, 114tl, 115tr, 119b); Mrs Ernest G. Kleinwort (front cover); Mrs Meanley (47t, 103r, 108br, 120l, 120r); students of Merrist Wood Agricultural College (Chelsea Show 1982) (99); Mr & Mrs M. C. S. Philips (66r, 99bl); Mr & Mrs S. Rimmer (77, 93, 94, 106l, 108bl, 110tr, 119tl); Mrs J. H. Robinson (Denmans) (107tr, 107b, 119tr); Mrs M. A. Selwood (Furzey Gardens) (31bl, 31br, 102l, 117b); David Stevens (gardens designed by) (47b, 99br); Mr & Mrs G. H. Thorp (67); Mr & Mrs F. S. Weir (59, 109); Director, Wisley Gardens, Surrey (13, 14, 15tr, 29, 51t, 55b, 112, 124l, 125l); Mrs White (60, 111, 115tl); Geoff and Faith Whiten (designed by) (44, 104tr); F. W. Woolworth Ltd (garden designed for) (101t).

Thanks are also due to the many other unknown gardeners whose public and private gardens have been featured in this book.

Picture credits
All the photographs in this book have been taken by the author with the exception of the following: page 45, Edwin H. Bradley Ltd (Bradstone); page 75, Stapeley Water Gardens; pages 46r, 47b, David Stevens. The author wishes to thank them for their help.

The line drawings and colour artwork are the work of Deborah Gandy.

Introduction

This is not a garden design book that will tell you how to create a wonderful garden by numbers, or more precisely by detailed plans for everything from paving to plants. If you want a ready-made garden, and can afford to carry out the plans, then you should consult a professional landscape architect or garden designer. This book is for the person who knows he can do better things with his garden but wants to know how, and who is keen to create an individual and personally designed garden but lacks the basic techniques or the ideas to achieve the results.

If you do want to follow a plan in detail, assuming you can adapt it to your plot of land, be wary of the problems. Your own garden may not be orientated the same way, and a plant that is in a sunny spot in a plan for someone else's garden may be in shade in yours. The plants chosen for perhaps an acid or neutral soil may not be suitable for your garden if the soil is chalky. Plans and ideas should form the basis of new ideas of your own. This book is primarily about ideas: tips for how to go about designing your garden, suggestions for dependable plants to include, and examples of what other gardeners have done. Take these three elements, add a little imagination, and there is no reason why you should not have a better garden, and one to be proud of.

Never think that you cannot do it, nor be deterred by the prospect of the creative aspects or of the work involved in carrying out the ideas. If you make a start, you have taken the biggest creative step, and the actual construction can be done in stages as time and money permit.

Plans and Priorities

Enthusiasm is a wonderful thing; it is what spurs us on to better things. When it comes to making a garden, however, it is easy to be carried away with a rush of impulsive ideas only to find the enthusiasm waning when the dream has to be translated into reality by physical hard work, and as the true financial cost dawns.

Even if you are fortunate enough to be free of financial constraints and are also able to employ someone to do the constructional work for you, enthusiasm alone, without the objective assessment to go with it, is hardly likely to lead to a well-planned garden.

There can be no ideal garden — only one that is right for you. If you are clear, however, about what you want from your garden, the chances are that you will get it right. That is the point at which you can let imagination and enthusiasm play their part.

Garden planning can be great fun, especially on a cold winter's day, when armchair gardening is so much more enticing than the real thing. Nevertheless, remember that no matter how good the plans are on paper the garden is both three-dimensional and living. The most work-able ideas probably come from standing outside and visualizing it in the mind's eye.

Most gardeners dream of a lawn like this as a setting for their plants, but a garden that looks as neat yet natural as this one demands time as well as careful early planning. It will need regular attention from spring to autumn, but the results are usually worth it.

1 Deciding What You Want

Start by listing your ideals. You will probably have to compromise in the light of what is practical or economically possible, but it is the only real starting point.

There are almost bound to be conflicting demands. Your interest may lie primarily in plants, yet if you have a family of young children it is almost as impossible to keep them off the 'flower' areas as it is to keep a cat off. Children, too, must have somewhere to play; to ban them from the garden is to miss an opportunity to generate an enthusiasm for plants and gardens. Even the needs of boisterous children and garden-loving adults *can* be accommodated together; it is a matter of planning for them in the design, as well as choosing tough plants (which does not mean that they are not also pretty), and plastic cloches and frames instead of glass.

Do not dismiss long-term ideals just because you cannot hope to achieve the results within a season. Gardening should be a pleasure rather than hard work, and there is nothing wrong with planning the work in stages over several years. It spreads both the work and the cost. In the meantime, you have at least made a start. If you do this, however, it makes sense to plant the trees and shrubs at an early stage.

Some of the Options

The checklist on page 10 will assist you in highlighting the features you want to incorporate into the design. There is an even more fundamental decision to be made first, and this depends on what type of gardener you are. If you are a plantsman, then you will be looking for as much planting space as possible, and probably as little concrete or paving; if you look on the garden more as an outdoor room to relax in, then the plants will probably be secondary to shape and form, the flesh on the skeleton. The overall visual impact will be the prime consideration.

Indeed, even if you are primarily a plant enthusiast it is wise to ignore specific plants when designing your garden, unless of course there are worthwhile specimen trees or shrubs that ought to be incorporated. It is for that reason that detailed planting lists are not given for the plans within this book. It matters little whether you plant, say, *Malus* 'John Downie' or *Malus* 'Golden Hornet'; both are fine plants and it is only a matter of personal preference. Equally you ought to plant to suit your soil; some of the gardens illustrated might make a feature of a rhododendron because the soil is acid, but on a chalky soil a syringa (lilac) might serve equally well.

Patios are very popular, but do not rush into paving purely on grounds of labour-saving. You can have a 'predominantly plants' garden that is still undemanding of time once it is established. It is simply a matter of choosing minimum-maintenance plants, probably with lots of ground cover. Some plants are well behaved; others, such as forget-me-nots and *Sedum acre*, you will come to regret introducing for years to come.

A paved area with containers, including window-boxes, is an ideal solution if you want plenty of replenishable colour with the minimum physical effort (although 'running costs' can be high with container gardening).

There are of course many other options; a low-maintenance 'natural' garden may appeal. This may be one where most of the grass can be left long among trees and shrubs, with lots of naturalized or wild flowers to brighten the scene according to season (*see* page 111). Alternatively, if the garden is not large enough for that, you can make a large pond the key feature.

Always bear in mind the maintenance aspect of the garden you create. If you are at home all the time it probably will not be a problem, but if you only have weekends (many of which will be wet) it becomes more critical.

As a guide to how labour-intensive various elements of the garden are likely to be, the following list may be useful.

For a *given area*, lawns are no more labour-intensive than the garden as a whole, even allowing for spiking, feeding and so on, as well as (power) mowing. The *same area* of bedding can take perhaps ten times as long to maintain, herbaceous borders perhaps twice as long. Of course beds and borders do not usually take up as much space as the lawn, and in any case a garden should be a balance. Hedges are also time-consuming, but the proportion of the garden that they occupy is normally very small, and they make a major contribution by providing shelter and a background for the rest of the garden.

Least time-consuming is rough grass, woodland, and ponds.

When deciding on the area of lawn that you can maintain, remember that a fairly coarse lawn, possibly with a few weeds in it, will require much less maintenance than one like that illustrated on p. 7.

Decide on your priorities first. The owner of this garden wanted to do away with the lawn and hedges, and keep to a minimum-maintenance design.

Checklist

Decorative features
Flower beds
Herb garden
Herbaceous borders
Lawn
Ornamental trees
Pergola
Rock garden
Shrub borders
Soft fruit
Terrace/patio
Top fruit
Vegetable plot

Practical features
Barbecue
Clothes line
Dustbin area
Garage
Greenhouse
Manhole cover disguise
Rotary drier
Sandpit
Summerhouse
Swimming pool
Swing
Tank/shed camouflage
Tool shed

2 Analysing the Restraints

Most of us have to live with some restraints. Sometimes it is the site or soil, but often it is time, money or physical effort.

Site is the most difficult to resolve, short of moving house! It is best regarded as a challenge, and best dealt with by the choice of suitable plants rather than structural change. A narrow passageway between two houses can be improved only marginally by suitable windbreaks (whether man-made or growing); it will probably remain a rather sunless and inhospitable place in which to grow plants. It may be best to use areas like this for dustbins and storage, or even tough plants such as privet if you need a hedge in such a place. Though often despised it will grow where many other subjects would perish.

Soil is less of a problem. Within limits you can make it more acid or more alkaline, and you can do much to improve its structure by good husbandry. If it really is too extreme to make much impression in this way, then the answer is simply to grow plants that thrive on chalk, peat, sand, clay or whatever the problem happens to be.

Time is always important. One only needs to see how quickly a well-kept garden 'goes wild' if neglected to realize that a garden cannot be left to its own devices; and it is no use hoping that paving will solve the problem, for plants in containers will soon look pathetic if regular watering, feeding and weeding is neglected.

Unless you have a motorized mower, keep lawns to a minimum, and unless you are able to cut them regularly they are best avoided completely. Remember, lawns need *regular* attention during the growing season. For a really neat finish you will have to trim the edges regularly too. Hedges obviously take up more time to maintain than walls or fences, but they have an aesthetic quality you may not be prepared to sacrifice, and of course they are cheaper. If you want a hedge, choose one that only needs an annual clip (*see* page 40).

Avoid annuals, as bedding is very demanding and hardy annuals need tedious thinning, and choose perennials that need little regular attention. That does not necessarily mean trees and large shrubs; there are many herbaceous plants that require no staking, are not invasive, and will grow to fill their allotted space with little special effort. Some will effectively smother weeds in the process.

*This spring scene is in a garden created on an unpromising chalky hillside.
Several famous gardens have been made on very difficult sites.*

Ground cover plants are especially useful because they reduce the
demand for weeding. They will need hacking back when they outgrow
their space, but this is a once-a-year job. If you have to leave the garden
unattended for periods, steer clear of vegetables; failure to thin at the
right time will lead to disappointment, and the whole exercise
becomes pointless if the crops are not harvested when they are ready.

Money is a restraint for many people. If it is just a short-term
embarrassment, the answer is to phase the construction over a period
of perhaps two or three years, and to raise most of your plants from
seed. Even trees and shrubs can be raised this way, and although you
need patience the end result is more satisfying than buying plants.

You can *combine utility with beauty. This fan-trained apple, which has rosy-red fruits, shows just how decorative some fruits can be.*

Sometimes, however, it is not just a matter of reducing expenditure on the garden, but actually of making the garden contribute to the household budget. The kitchen garden then becomes the first priority. Nevertheless the garden need never be dull. A *neat* vegetable plot can be a picture, and a herb ·bed can be a real garden feature. With imagination vegetables can also be used decoratively; carrots and beetroot make charming plants for a border, and cardoons make really majestic plants if you have space.

Fan-trained or espalier cherries, grapes, apples and peaches can make a super display, both attractive and mouthwatering.

Physical effort is a problem for many gardeners, whether through

Age or infirmity are handicaps enough without being deprived of the pleasures of gardening. Raised beds may be the answer.

age or ill health. Fortunately there is no reason why they should not enjoy their garden to the full, though raised beds and special tools can add to the expense.

It is in a garden for the disabled or not-so-strong that planning really pays dividends. This is especially so if a wheelchair has to be used. It goes without saying that steps should be avoided, any change in height being achieved by raised beds if possible. There is absolutely no reason, however, why raised beds *have* to be incorporated. The picture on p. 10 shows a minimum-maintenance garden.

Unless you want to grow perhaps a few salad crops in a small bed, vegetables are not a viable proposition, as annual digging really is a necessity (good results are sometimes claimed by the 'no digging' school, but the amounts of compost required are substantial, and the 'deep bed' system calls for a special layout to avoid walking on the beds). If you want to contribute to the family budget, it is best to do so with a few carefully chosen and trained fruit trees instead.

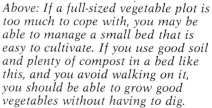

Above: If a full-sized vegetable plot is too much to cope with, you may be able to manage a small bed that is easy to cultivate. If you use good soil and plenty of compost in a bed like this, and you avoid walking on it, you should be able to grow good vegetables without having to dig.

Top right: Fruit trees, like this espalier-trained pear, will look attractive and amply earn their keep.

Right: A garden planned for retirement. Neat, distinctive, and minimum-maintenance.

Finally, remember that the answer to your particular problem may lie in one of the aids available to make difficult jobs easier, rather than elaborate replanning.

The Law and Your Neighbours

Most of the changes you make to your garden are unlikely to affect your neighbours or the local planning authority, but it is as well to remember that you are unlikely to be able to do just *anything* with your own garden. The comments on this page apply to the UK, but similar rules apply in other countries. You cannot necessarily remove all the trees in your garden, for instance. It is just possible that some of them may have tree preservation orders on them if they are particularly interesting or environmentally useful. This is unlikely with small trees, but if you are in doubt check with your local council (ask for the planning office). You can obtain permission to fell in certain circumstances (if it is dangerous for instance) but you must replant with another tree of the same species (unless you can negotiate to the contrary).

The deeds of your house may also stipulate restrictions (on the size and siting of fences and hedges for instance). Even if the deeds do not place such restrictions on you, local byelaws or the highways department may stop you; particularly if what you do could restrict the view for drivers. It is even possible that you may run into trouble if you alter the access from your garden into a main road (or one near a bend or road junction). If your plans are likely to run into difficulties on any of these counts it is well worth checking first. The planning office of your local council will usually be helpful on these matters.

Most free-standing sheds, summerhouses and greenhouses away from a boundary are unlikely to fall foul of building regulations or planning permission, but again it is worth a telephone call to check.

It is also wise to remember the moral obligation to neighbours in what you do. Changing the position of a flower bed is hardly likely to involve your neighbours, but knocking down a fence, building a wall, planting a potentially large tree against a boundary or draining your land in such a way that it could affect the water table in the next garden all affect your neighbours. You owe it to them to discuss your plans with them first. They may not be able to stop you anyway but at least you have shown the courtesy of asking, and will know how they feel about it. If there are objections you will have to balance the benefits of that part of your plan against the inconvenience of upsetting your neighbours.

3 Planning for the Future

Many gardeners make a new garden late in life, often shortly before or after retirement. Designing a garden at this time calls for realism. With each advancing year bending and barrowing is likely to become more difficult. If you design it with minimum maintenance in mind it is less likely to become a chore and a worry with passing time.

Again it does not mean that the garden need not be horticulturally interesting. A heather and conifer garden may take a bit of weeding for the first few years, but then it will need little more than an annual trimming, yet it can provide interest and variety throughout the year. A collection of small garden trees and a few choice shrubs, whether set in grass or paving, can provide an increasing delight as each year the plants mature, with little day-to-day attention.

It is not only older gardeners who need to plan ahead. The newly married have many demands on time, children need somewhere to play, and money may be short. Gradually, however, children grow up, and money tends to become less of a problem. Time, resources and common sense dictate that the garden must meet the immediate needs, but that does not mean that the future cannot be borne in mind too.

Frequently, of course, the first or second house only serve as temporary stepping stones to better things. There are still many, however, who live in family homes where there are natural ties, and it is in these cases that it makes sense to plan and plant with the future in mind.

It is best to start with your ideal garden, then decide which parts can serve as play areas, and so on, to be converted at a later stage. If you decide where the major plants, such as trees, are to go, these can be planted immediately so that they will make substantial specimens by the time the garden takes its final form.

4 Making a Start

Writing it Down

Inspiration seldom comes without stimulation, and the best way to stimulate ideas is to get something down on paper. You do not have to be an artist to produce a good garden design, just as you do not have to have good handwriting to write a good novel. If you start to concentrate too much on making a neat job of your initial efforts on paper the chances are that you will fail to create an inspired overall plan. It is nice, of course, to produce a neatly finished final job; just do not let unnecessary constraints inhibit the free flow of ideas initially.

A clipboard is invaluable, simply because it is so useful to be able to wander into the garden as you are working, to visualize or resolve a problem on the spot. Sheets of graph paper are not essential, but they make life a lot easier, especially for the finished plan. Rules are obviously helpful even for rough plans, while in the garden a long, retractable surveying linen tape is very useful. If you feel that you are not likely to use this much afterwards and you want to avoid the cost, you can manage quite well with measuring sticks (marked off in say 30 cm or 1 ft intervals). This method, however, is more likely to give you backache.

If you have a compass you might find it useful, but most people have a good idea of where the south lies in relation to their house.

Making a Shortlist

Before attempting to work out the design, be clear about what you want to achieve (*see* checklist on page 10), and analyse what you are likely to be able to achieve within the plan. Where space is unlimited, and you have resources to match, there will not be a lot to stand in your way, but often it is not possible to incorporate all the features that you would like. Make a water garden too small, for instance, and it will look mean and be difficult to manage well. It is better to keep to a few bold features to give the garden a sense of purpose. Rank your desirable features in some sort of priority, perhaps marking them A, B, C. Design the garden around the A features, then try to incorporate the Bs. C features should be introduced only if they can be added without jeopardizing the overall plan so far.

Almost as important as the features you would like to introduce are the assets the garden already possesses. Do not hesitate to 'grub up' (remove) unwanted shrubs and trees if they are of no ornamental value, but never do so without careful thought. Established shrubs, and especially trees, do so much to give a garden a sense of maturity that it is always wise to try to incorporate at least some of them. In the case of large or special interest trees, bear in mind that occasionally they may have a preservation order on them.

If you do have to have a large tree cut down (a job for a professional tree surgeon) it may be possible to use the stump to make some form of feature, such as a seat.

Garden sheds, greenhouses and the like can be moved, but it is more convenient if they can be incorporated without the need for resiting.

Make a note of the practical elements to be incorporated: provision for dustbins, bunkers or storage tanks, and basic paths. Paths can be a particular problem as there is often a conflict between the need for wide practical paths in straight lines, and aesthetic considerations. The prospect of moving an existing concrete path, or mortared paving slabs, is a daunting one indeed; but unless they fortunately happen to be in the right place do not let the paths dictate the whole layout of the garden, which they tend to do. On the whole, rotary clothes driers are less obtrusive than conventional lines, but this need not always be so (especially if you are prepared to take the line down when it is not in use).

Sometimes paths and drives just have to run in straight lines, but you can do much to improve the harsh lines by using suitable plants along the edges, where they will not receive direct wear. The plant in the foreground in this picture is Polygonum affine.

Try to avoid too many straight lines in a small front garden. The ribbon effect of the pedestrian path and the drive to the garage makes the garden on the left very uninteresting. A simple and inexpensive change to the existing design (right) may be all that is necessary to give it more 'character'.

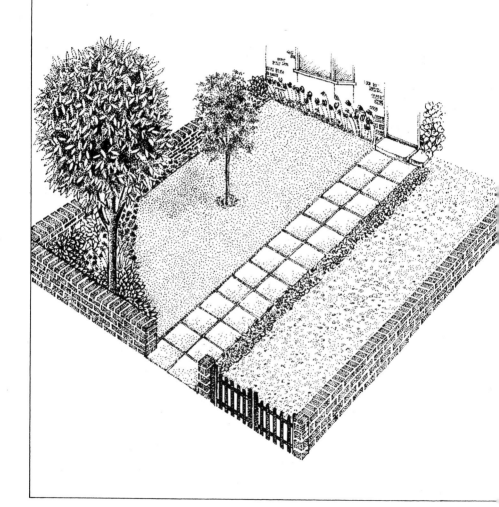

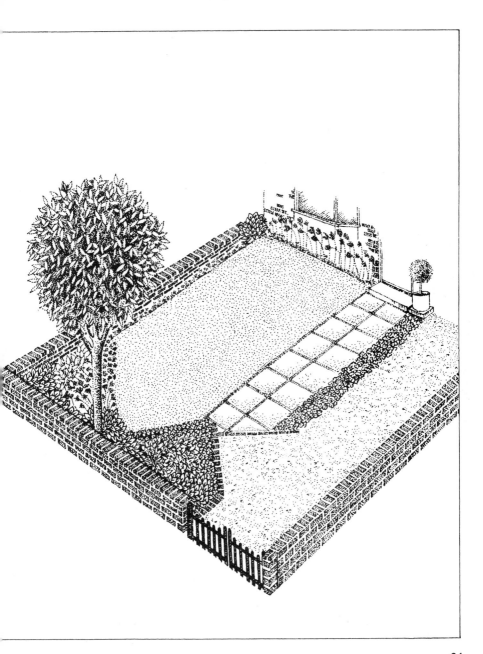

5 Drawing up the Plan

Aspect should be taken into account when deciding on the position of a patio or other sitting-out area. Ideally it ought to face south, although you will also get plenty of afternoon sun to enjoy if it faces west.

Aspect should also be considered when siting large trees and shrubs as you do not want too much shadow to be cast in the wrong places. Shade is very nice on a hot summer's day, but there are likely to be more days when you would be better without it.

Flowers, and vegetables too, will almost always grow better in an open, sunny situation. Try to use the shadiest spots for garden sheds, paths, dustbins, the compost heap, and so on.

You will find it much easier to draw the outline of the garden, together with key features to be retained, clearly on a piece of graph paper, and use tracing-paper overlays to rough out your various plans. It will save a lot of tedious redrawing of the outlines if you do not get it right first time (which is unlikely).

It is usually more convenient to do a rough freehand sketch first, with key dimensions written in, later transferring this to graph paper indoors. If your plans are likely to be simple and you do not have to be too precise, you may prefer to pace out the areas, but for accuracy you should use a measuring tape.

Start with the house, indicating the position of doors and windows, then work out the boundaries; if the garden is rectangular this is simple enough but gardens of irregular shape may have to be triangulated. It sounds an off-putting business, but is really quite simple once you know how. The example on p. 24 demonstrates the principle. To find the position and distance of point X on your plan, simply measure from here to two points in a known position (in this case A and B on the house), and transfer these to the plan as scale measurements. For example, if you are using 5 mm ($\frac{1}{5}$ in) to 30 cm (1 ft) as a scale, and point X is 9 m (30 ft) from point B and 6 m (20 ft) from point A, these would be 150 mm (6 in) and 100 mm (4 in) respectively on your plan. Use a pair of compasses and mark arcs at these distances. Where the two intersect is point X. The same principle can be used for determining the position of anything within the garden. If the tree in the example illustrated is 3 m (10 ft) from A and 4.5 m (15 ft) from B your arcs will be made at 50 mm (2 in) and 75 mm (3 in) respectively; where they intersect pinpoints the position of the tree.

Changes in height are not easy to incorporate into your plan unless you draw one in profile too, and you may be content to make a note in the margin of the approximate rise and fall (in centimetres rather than rate of incline). Remember, you are not preparing official plans but a guide for yourself, and you will in any case peg out the plan afterwards to see how it looks. Things never look quite as they appeared on paper.

Once you have the basic plan roughed out, transfer it to graph paper. The size of your garden and the type of graph paper used must dictate the scale you adopt; two squares to 30 cm (1 ft) or ten squares to 1 m (3 ft) is often convenient.

Fix the background plan to your clipboard, and a sheet of tracing paper over this. Try to decide on the focal point(s) first and work towards these, incorporating your priority features (As) on your list, first. The other features can be incorporated as the plan develops. Do not try to include anything for the sake of it: bold simple lines usually work better than a hotch-potch of features.

If the garden is small, try to embrace in the design a large, open area (lawn or paving) without dividing it up too much. A large garden will usually benefit from being broken up into elements, though it is always useful to retain a line to a distant focal point to hold the design together.

It will help you to visualise the main changes to your garden if you can mark them out first. A hosepipe is useful for indicating sweeping borders, and trees and other key plants can be indicated by stakes. Leave them in place long enough to observe shadows, and try to view from as many angles as possible.

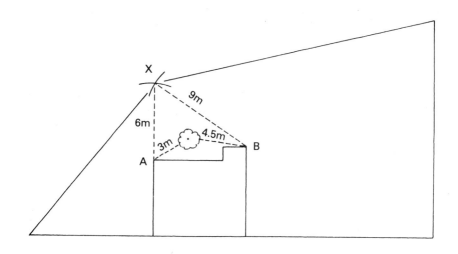

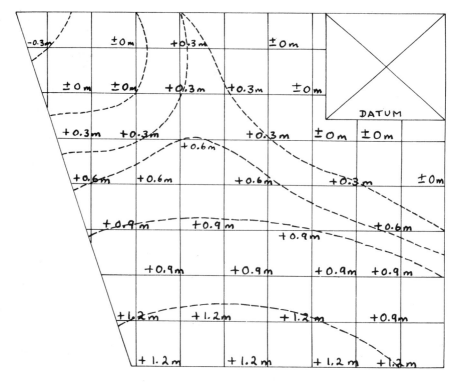

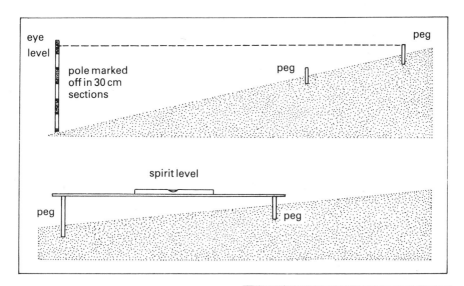

Opposite, top: If your garden has an irregular shape, fixing key points on your plan can be difficult unless you 'triangulate'. This is not as complicated as it sounds (see page 22 for an explanation of how it works).

Opposite, below: To draw a contour map (which may not be necessary), take levels at regular intervals and transfer them to your plan. Then go into the garden to complete your contour lines by eye using the grid as a guide.

Above: If the area is large you can take your level readings at quite large intervals, using pegs at set points and a siting pole. If the area is small, you may be able to work with a straight-edge and spirit-level.

Right: Try to peg out your plan in the garden — only then will you get the right three-dimensional effect.

If you are pleased with your first efforts you are lucky. Be prepared to try alternative plans, even if you go back to the first one after all. At least you will have explored more possibilities. Do not worry too much about the plants at this stage; it is important to know whether you are to incorporate a water garden or a rockery, but of little consequence which plants you eventually grow in them.

Testing the Plan

Never be satisfied with a garden plan without testing it out first, *before* you order materials. It does not take long to mark out paths and beds with canes and string, and this will give you an impression of scale that is seldom possible from a paper plan unless you have years of experience.

You can use lime or sand to mark out areas, and even a hosepipe can prove useful for providing a curved bed. For rectangular areas, string stretched between canes is useful.

Specimen trees or important tall plants can be indicated by long canes or poles.

At this stage pay particular attention to the width and curvature of paths. Check that beds and borders are of a workable size (and that you can easily reach across with a hoe) and that curves are not unnaturally tight.

The view from an upstairs window will usually give a useful semi-plan impression.

Leave the markers in position for a day, and observe whether shadows are likely to cause any problems.

When you are satisfied with the framework, you can make a start on the construction, and spend the evenings deciding on the plants to incorporate, which is one of the most exciting parts of the job.

Deciding Who Does What

Sometimes time or the physical effort involved in translating the plan into reality act as a restraint to good design, particularly if the prospect of employing a contractor to do it for you is likely to upset the bank manager.

If you employ someone to do it all for you, it will be expensive, as labour is not cheap. Nevertheless, you may be prepared to leave some of the heavy or more skilled construction jobs to a professional, and do the rest yourself as a compromise.

The structural work, such as walls, pools and paving, is known as hard landscaping. These are the jobs that you are most likely to need help with, although they are all well within the scope of the average gardener with the time and ability to tackle the physical aspects.

The soft landscaping, the lawn, planting trees, shrubs and other plants, is something most of us enjoy doing ourselves.

Many of the jobs can, of course, be made easier with the right tools. A concrete mixer can be particularly useful, and this can be hired. If there is a lot of rough ground to be cultivated, you can save a lot of time and effort initially by hiring a cultivator.

Removing large trees and stumps is certainly a job for the professional. If you do decide to bring in help, be sure to ask for an estimate of cost, and do not hesitate to ask for clarification of any detail that you are not sure about.

You may prefer to use a contractor that belongs to one of the landscape contractor associations. You may get a perfectly satisfactory job done, possibly at less cost, by someone who is not a member, but it is as well to be cautious and try to speak to someone who has had a job done by him before committing yourself.

Removing an old hedge can help to transform a garden — but it is extremely hard work best done by a contractor with the right equipment.

27

Garden Features

The initial planning should be concerned primarily with shapes and patterns, and the allocation of basic features. Once you have decided on the features you want to incorporate you can then consider the form they are to take. It is one thing to decide on a hedge instead of a fence or wall, but quite another to resolve which one to plant. For a paved area you might use bricks or natural or man-made paving slabs. Even if you decide on man-made slabs, perhaps because of cost, there is a bewildering array of shapes and sizes from which to choose (not to mention colours). It is in these areas that you can gain most from seeing what other people have done. Look at some of the options (in this book and in the gardens that you see) and decide what is right for your taste and your garden.

Always remember the effect of weather. Paving slabs and rockery stones can take on an entirely different appearance once they have been weathered. You almost need a pair of sunglasses to look at newly quarried tufa rock in sunlight, yet it weathers to a very natural and unobtrusive shade.

The object of this part of the book is to give you ideas for various treatments, and show you how they will look in a mature setting.

Do not be afraid to mix materials. Cobbles set in concrete are particularly effective in breaking up an otherwise monotonous area, and they help by adding 'texture' to the garden.

6 Paths and Drives

So often in unplanned gardens the path follows a straight line to the front door or an equally straight line from the back door along the length of the clothes-line. On the other hand most paths have to be practical, and if the way to your front door takes a meandering course the chances are that everyone from the paperboy to the milkman will decide on a short cut. A gentle curve or an L-shaped approach, perhaps from a drive for the car, are sensible alternatives. A useful tip for preventing visitors cutting the corner at a right-angled junction or turn is to introduce an area of cobbles or small boulders as part of the design. At least they will stand the wear!

Width is equally important. A 'strolling' path, perhaps stepping stones through flower beds, or to a feature such as a pond or seat, can be narrow. Practical paths to the front door, washing line or garden shed should be wide enough to take two people abreast. It is a little disconcerting for visitors to have to approach your front door Indian-file.

Left: A herringbone path helps to create a 'cottage garden' atmosphere.

Above right: A complicated design, calling for the use of half-bricks in the centre. The bricks laid 'on edge' at the sides give a neat finish, but you need a lot of them. It is probably only worth making a path as complex as this if it forms a key feature of the garden.

Above far right: Even flagstones can look good with an edging of bricks.

Right: Natural stone is expensive, and it looks best used generously. It has a mellow appearance, but it can be uneven to walk on.

Far right: Modern materials should not be dismissed — they can look right even in a very natural setting.

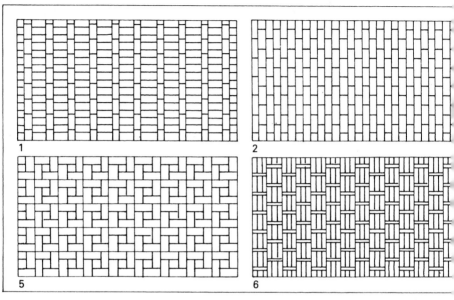

Below: Gravel is very 'sympathetic' and perfect for curved paths.

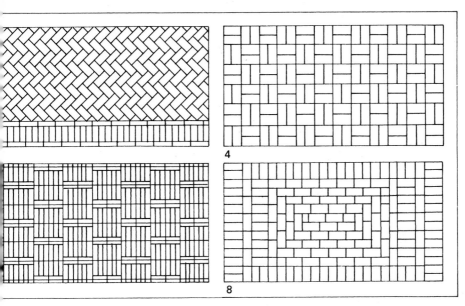

Above: Brick patterns. 1, 2, 5, 6, and 7 are effective for a large area, and 8 for an isolated rectangle. For fairly narrow paths 3 or 4 are suitable.

Below: Circular paving stones infilled with cobbles set in concrete.

33

The practical considerations resolved, you can turn to the aesthetic aspect.

For drives used by cars the choice lies primarily between paving, *in situ* concrete, or gravel. An expanse of concrete, or even asphalt, seldom looks attractive.

Gravel is very useful because it blends in with the garden setting, and a gravel drive can be curved in a natural sweep that is difficult to achieve well with paving. Its drawback is that it is hard to walk on and noisy to drive over. Again it is worth considering a compromise where the drive is straight: lay strips of paving within the gravelled area to provide tracks for the wheels of vehicles and a 'softer' alternative for pedestrians.

For paths that are to take nothing heavier than a wheelbarrow or a lawnmower, the choice is much wider.

Grass paths are useful for linking one area of lawn with another, or even between areas in the vegetable garden; but avoid them where they are likely to receive a lot of heavy wear. Remember that they are also labour-intensive to maintain. There is the regular cutting, and a lot of edges to trim.

For hard wear and comfort, especially if you have to use it for barrows and the like, a hard surface is best. Paving is useful for straight lines, but not so easy to lay to a curve (you can fill in the gaps with gravel or cobbles, but it ceases to be a smooth path for pushing things along).

If you do decide on paving, try to avoid too many mixed colours unless it happens to link a matching patio.

Brick is an ideal material; it is both hard-wearing and attractive in a garden setting. There are many alternative patterns that can be used to add interest (*see* pp. 32-3). Bricks can also be laid in a curve quite easily without the gaps being too conspicuous.

Gravel is most effective used in broad, sweeping paths, and can make a splendid setting for plants. With modern weedkillers, weeds should not be a problem.

Crazy-paving presents one with the choice of whether to concrete between the slabs or to grow plants between some of the cracks. Suitable plants, that will tolerate being crushed occasionally by a boot, do look charming, but rule out the use of weedkillers on the rest of the path. They are also best avoided where there is likely to be a lot of wear, and in such places it is best to concrete the gaps.

As a word of warning, crazy-paving can look superb with natural stone in a cottage garden setting but very contrived in a modern garden, especially if broken, coloured paving stones are used.

Stepping stone paths can look really charming, but they must have a sense of purpose. They should lead somewhere, if only to a garden seat, the pond, or to the compost heap situated behind some shrubs. If the path just zig-zags aimlessly with no sense of direction, it will look contrived.

If the stones can lead purposefully across water *en route*, so much the better. Rectangular or round paving slabs let into the lawn or soil are popular, but sawn logs are especially attractive leading off through a border or shrubbery.

Steps

A change of level always adds interest, but steps should be shallow, and whenever possible an alternative route provided with a slope if lawnmowers and wheelbarrows are likely to be required.

A change in level does not have to be steep to create interest. Here the step has been brought out to make it a more positive feature.

7 Fences, Walls, Gates

There is a tendency, especially on new housing estates, to go for open plan designs. Indeed, there may be restrictions to erecting fences or walls in such areas written into the deeds. Nevertheless the need for privacy is almost universally acknowledged, in the back garden at least.

If you live in rolling countryside you may want to consider a ha-ha at the end (an old device used by some of our great landscape architects of the past). For most of us, however, it is a matter of settling for a hedge or fence. For front gardens, low walls are another attractive option, though cost usually rules out a high wall at the back.

Hedges, discussed on pages 40 and 41, have the merit of being comparatively inexpensive to plant but are much more labour-intensive to maintain than a fence or wall.

Wooden fences provide an efficient means of providing some privacy quickly. The result is instant, and not obtrusive once there is a covering of plants. Do not expect it to last for ever, however. Many kinds will begin to look tatty and gaps open up between the laps after perhaps five years or so. Wooden posts have a tendency to rot (although metal post-holders are helpful here). Concrete posts are not pretty but they are practical.

There is a wide range of styles from which to choose, and much depends on the setting. A picket fence can look superb in a cottage garden or country setting, but quite out of place on a modern housing estate.

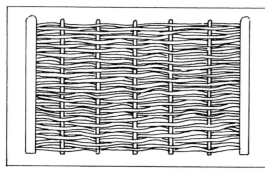

Wattle hurdles *are not particularly attractive as a boundary fence, but can be useful for screening areas within the garden, perhaps the compost heap or kitchen garden.*

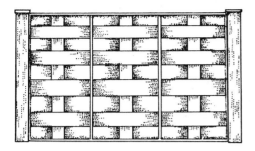

Interwoven panels *give a good degree of privacy, but are not peep-proof, and the strips tend to distort with age.*

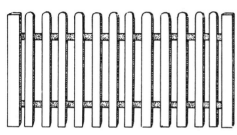

Picket *fencing can look charming in the right setting and painted white. It goes well with 'cottage' gardens.*

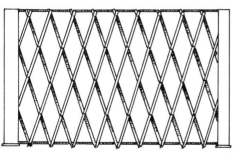

Trellis panels *can be used to provide support for suitable plants, but bear in mind that they are seldom robust enough to have a long life. They will be subject to considerable stresses in high winds once they are covered with plants.*

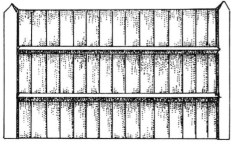

Close-board *fencing is strong, long-lasting, and gives good privacy if the height is sufficient.*

Walls are neat, fairly unobtrusive if not too high, and maintenance-free. Brick or 'stone' walls can be provided with a planting cavity, so they can even provide a blaze of colour too.

The garden gate is fast disappearing, but it can be quite a pleasant feature. Even if the front garden is not a suitable place, it is nice to have a gate perhaps at the side of the house. It serves a dual function of providing a sense of privacy and engendering a sense of exploration as you open it to enter another part of the garden.

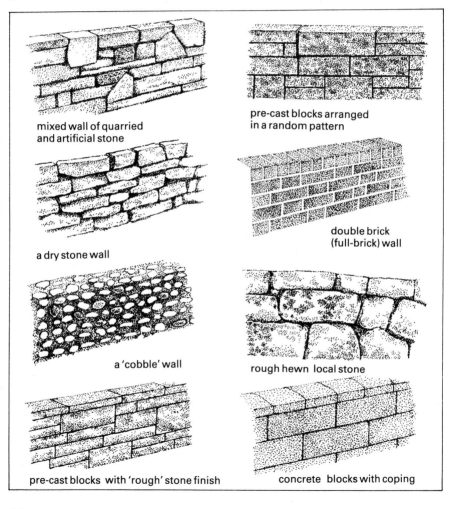

mixed wall of quarried and artificial stone

pre-cast blocks arranged in a random pattern

a dry stone wall

double brick (full-brick) wall

a 'cobble' wall

rough hewn local stone

pre-cast blocks with 'rough' stone finish

concrete blocks with coping

Right: Walls can be made more interesting if they have a planting cavity. Rock plants and bedding plants are usually planted, but here dwarf conifers have been used. They are Juniperus communis *'Compressa'*, Thuja orientalis *'Aurea Nana'*, and Chamaecyparis lawsoniana *'Minima Glauca'*.

Below: If your garden borders open countryside, you could try the old idea of a ha-ha — a barrier that does not block the view. It does not have to be on a large scale.

8 Hedges

Hedges are often taken for granted, yet they provide a backcloth for the garden as well as a practical boundary marker. Be clear about some of the myths before deciding whether or not to plant a hedge.

They do need more attention than walls or fences, but often a once-a-year trim is sufficient; it is the ubiquitous privet that has given many other hedges a bad name.

20 Useful Hedging Plants

Name	No. of cuts	Best height	Planting distance	Relative cost	
Berberis darwinii Darwin's barberry	1 (after flowering)	1.2-1.8 m (4-6 ft)	60 cm (2 ft)	Medium	
Berberis thunbergii 'Atropurpurea' Thunberg's barberry	1 (after flowering)	0.6-1.2 m (2-4 ft)	45 cm (1½ ft)	Medium	
Berberis stenophylla	1 (after flowering)	1.2-1.8 m (4-6 ft)	60 cm (2 ft)	Medium	
Chamaecyparis lawsoniana 'Green Hedger'	1 (August)	1.5-2.4 m* (5-8 ft)*	60 cm (2 ft)	High	
Cotoneaster lacteus	1 (summer)	2.4 m (8 ft)	60 cm (2 ft)	Medium	
Cotoneaster simonsii	1 (July)	0.9-1.5 m (3-5 ft)	45 cm (1½ ft)	Medium	
× *Cupressocyparis leylandii*	1 (August)	1.5-2.4 m* (5-8 ft)*	60 cm (2 ft)	High	
Escallonia Chilean gum	1 (after flowering)	1.2-1.8 m (4-6 ft)	45 cm (1½ ft)	Medium	
Fagus sylvatica Beech	1 (August)	1.5-2.4 m* (5-8 ft)*	45 cm (1½ ft)	Low	
Forsythia intermedia	2 (after flowering; light shaping August)	1.2-1.8 m (4-6 ft)	60 cm (2 ft)	Medium	
Lavandula spica Lavender	1 (after flowering)	45-60 cm (1½-2 ft)	30-45 cm (1-1½ ft)	Low	

continued on p. 42

Planting a hedge is usually cheaper than buying a fence of the same length, but prices vary widely. Some hedging plants are twice as expensive as others, and for any particular kind you will pay a lot for an extra season's growth. Choose small plants, which are cheaper and will probably catch up the larger plants in a surprisingly short time. The accompanying table gives a guide to hedging plants.

Do not overlook the varied uses of hedging plants. The dwarf kinds such as lavender can make a useful low edging to an open-style garden. For informal hedges, perhaps between modern town gardens, some of the following hedges such as forsythia can be useful, whereas at the other extreme some of the hedging plants such as beech or × *Cupressocyparis leylandii* can be used to provide tall screens (they must be planted further apart if they are required as screens).

Remarks
Evergreen, flowers and foliage.
Foliage.
Evergreen, flowers.
Forms impenetrable barrier.
Evergreen. Good screen and barrier.
Evergreen, flowers, berries.
Informal.
Orange berries, pink flowers.
Partially evergreen.
Evergreen. Good screen and barrier.
Evergreen. Flowers. Neat.
Useful by sea, but not suitable for cold districts.
Though deciduous, dead leaves hang till spring. Makes useful barrier and screen.
Flowers. Informal.
Formal, flowering.

It may not seem obvious to have both a hedge and a wall, but a low wall like this one can help to fill in the occasional bareness at the base where the plants are grown sufficiently wide apart to be appreciated as individual specimens.

41

20 Useful Hedging Plants continued

Name	No. of cuts	Best height	Planting distance	Relative cost
Ligustrum ovalifolium 'Aureum' Golden privet	4 (May to August)	0.6-1.2 m (2-4 ft)	30-45 cm ($1-1\frac{1}{2}$ ft)	Medium
Lonicera nitida 'Fertilis' Shrubby honeysuckle	4 (May to August)	0.6-1.2 m (2-4 ft)	30-45 cm ($1-1\frac{1}{2}$ ft)	Low
Prunus 'Cistena' Crimson dwarf	1 (July or August)	0.9-1.2 m (3-4 ft)	30 cm (1 ft)	Medium
Prunus laurocerasus Laurel	1 (July or August)	1.5-1.8 m (5-6 ft)	45 cm ($1\frac{1}{2}$ ft)	Medium
Prunus pissardii Purple plum	2 (April and July)	1.2-1.8 m (4-6 ft)	45-60 cm ($1\frac{1}{2}$-2 ft)	Medium
Rosa 'Penelope'	1 (spring)	1.2-1.8 m (4-6 ft)	45-60 cm ($1\frac{1}{2}$-2 ft)	Medium
Spiraea × *arguta* Bridal wreath	1 (after flowering)	1.2-1.5 m (4-5 ft)	45-60 cm ($1\frac{1}{2}$-2 ft)	Medium
Taxus bacata Yew	1 (August)	1.2-1.8 m* (4-6 ft)	45-60 cm ($1\frac{1}{2}$-2 ft)	High
Thuja plicata 'Atrovirens'	1 (August)	1.5-2.4 m* (5-8 ft)*	45-60 cm ($1\frac{1}{2}$-2 ft)	High

* will grow considerably higher as a screen (should be planted at greater spacing for this)

Remarks

Foliage. Evergreen.

Evergreen formal hedge.
Good barrier.

Bright crimson leaves. Formal.

Evergreen. Foliage.
Good screen and barrier.
Copper-red leaves. White flowers
early spring. Formal.
Pale pink flowers. Informal.

Flowering, informal.

Evergreen conifer. Formal.
Very good barrier.
Evergreen conifer.

Opposite page, left: Although the green privet is often despised, the golden form can make a most attractive hedge. It also has the advantage of being slower-growing than the green kind.

Opposite page, right: Lavender makes a low, informal flowering hedge — fragrant and colourful in flower.

Below left: Once they are established, suitable roses can make a superb informal flowering hedge.

Below: Spiraea × arguta. *Although not a good barrier, it makes a splendid sight in May.*

9 Patios & Paved Areas

Patios are very popular, and few garden designs seem to lack at least a small paved area. You can always sit out on a lawn, of course, but a terrace or patio provides a natural link between the home and garden, and it provides a clean walking and sitting-out area regardless of weather. If the patio also has some form of roof shelter, the area really does become an extension of the home into the garden.

Design-wise a paved area can also form a gradual and more acceptable transition from building to garden. The main point to watch is

So many patios are flat and rectangular, yet with imagination you can get away from both these limitations even in a small area. This kind of treatment immediately lifts it out of the ordinary.

size in relation to the whole garden. If the paved area is too large, the garden is likely to look uninteresting, with too much concrete and not enough plants. If it is too small it can look mean and pointless. In a small garden say 10 m × 10 m (33 ft × 33 ft) or less, it is probably best to pave the whole area (allowing for beds and containers) or to keep it to an absolute minimum (hard paving round the house to provide access is obviously important). If you try to pave perhaps a third or half of an area like this, the amount of garden left will look paltry and the patio pretentious.

The patio is traditionally placed next to the house, leading into the garden. This is sensible, but do not follow convention too slavishly. If the site is sunless, it may be better to extend it from the house along one side of the garden, or even place it at the opposite end.

Choice of material will make a big difference to appearance. Modern pre-cast slabs look perfectly satisfactory in the setting of a modern building; but natural stone (expensive) or mellow bricks will usually produce a far better effect with an older home and in an informal garden.

The small interlocking concrete blocks, quite often seen in public places, should not be dismissed. They blend in well with both modern and traditional settings.

Some modern pre-cast paving slabs are made to look like classical designs, and these also look effective in almost any setting. They can be arranged to provide circular beds.

If using the popular coloured paving stones, try to see an area that has weathered.

Paving should not be seen in isolation. A flat expanse of hard surface running into a flat lawn can be very uninspiring. If you are on a sloping site the problem is to some extent solved, as you can form a terrace with a low wall to overlook a garden that slopes away. If it slopes up, you can introduce a few steps to lead into the garden proper, and plant up the retaining wall where you have cut into the slope to provide a colourful display of flowers.

On a flat site you can sometimes introduce a water feature that provides a useful link, or a low cavity wall that can be planted to be viewed from both sides.

Do not overlook the possibility of introducing a built-in seat. It produces a more integrated appearance, and an array of patio furniture standing out more or less permanently is not everyone's idea of an attractive sight.

Above: This small patio has been designed to act as a stepping off point for the rest of the garden, which is on a sloping site.

Far left: Sometimes a spot away from the house can give the most suitable view or setting for a patio.

Left: You can make a patio the main feature, in which case you will probably have to add things like raised beds and a pool to generate sufficient interest.

Right: Containers add height, but do not overdo them unless you can water and attend to them regularly.

10 Ornaments

There are some gardeners who cannot resist the temptation to fill their garden with gnomes and pixies. To another gardener these would be anathema. Some of the major gardens modelled on the classical Italian style make much of statuary, yet these seem almost universally admired. It is probably all a matter of scale and taste.

In most gardens of small or medium size, the key function of a statue or garden ornament is to provide a focal point. In a large garden there might be a natural vista, or a magnificent specimen tree to take the eye to a particular part of the garden. On the smaller scale (and even within small areas of a large garden), some other means has to be found. Often a water feature will do this, but a sundial or a well-chosen ornament can work equally well.

Design is very much a matter of personal taste (you are the one who

has to live with it), but position the colour so that it shows off to advantage. Bronze soon darkens, so it is best set in an open situation with a light background, perhaps grass. Marble and light-coloured materials are seen to advantage against dark greens, perhaps yew.

Bronze and marble are expensive of course, but you can buy stone or glass-fibre models more reasonably. Many of these are reproductions of classical designs, but do not be put off by something simple and modern. A bird, for instance, positioned on a pedestal and backed by a dark hedge, or ivy-covered wall, can be most striking.

Statues and ornaments not only need the right setting, but the right base too. Those that come complete with a base should still have a concrete foundation to stand on, set just beneath ground level. For small pieces it is often possible to build a brick or stone plinth to match other materials used in the garden.

Do not overlook garden ornaments other than statues, which can achieve the same object. A bird-bath or bird-table can be a useful focal point, and attract birds to the garden. Even a large ornamental container filled with plants can be all that is required.

11 The Rock Garden

If you are a real alpine enthusiast you would probably like to turn the whole of your garden into a miniature gorge. In fact even a small rock garden is not cheap or easy to construct well.

The best rock gardens are built on a naturally sloping site, preferably one that receives a good deal of sunshine. If you are fortunate enough to have such a site, a rock garden can make a super feature. The problem comes on flat sites, when the temptation to try to make the best of a bad situation often leads to a 'currants in a cake' appearance.

To work well, 'island' rock gardens need to be on a large scale; which is why they are sometimes seen to work well in local authority

gardens. Generally it is better to look at some of the alternative ways to enjoy rock plants if you do not have much space.

Rock and water gardens associate well together, especially with cascades (which again require a slope). On a flat site a bog garden may be a better companion to a pond.

There are alternatives if the site does not lend itself to a proper rock garden. A fairly flat scree bed, covered with fine gravel or stone chippings, can look most effective. A few rocks or large boulders can be incorporated to add interest, and dwarf conifers can bring a little extra height.

Suitable walls can provide plenty of planting space for rock plants, and low raised rock beds are another possibility.

If you are prepared to confine your plants to the choicer kinds, and avoid the rampant ones, you can make an attractive rock feature against the wall of a brick-based greenhouse; a rock such as tufa is ideal.

Left: What can be done in a few days if you have the money and the labour. Although this rock garden looks established and years old, it was built for the 1982 Chelsea show. Rocks as large as these need professional handling.

Right: Tufa is a much easier rock to handle. When dry it is comparatively light, and even a small amount can support a wide range of plants, and look natural.

Below right: A small flat site is difficult to handle successfully. It is best not to attempt a high, unnatural mound, and to keep the emphasis on the plants rather than the rocks.

12 The Water Garden

Water has a universal appeal and as a garden feature seldom fails to attract attention.

If you have small children it is a feature you may prefer to omit, or at least allow for but defer construction for a few years. The attraction for a toddler is even greater than for adults.

The shapes and sizes of garden pools is infinitely varied. The first decision, however, is whether it should be formal or informal in style.

For patios and gardens with fairly regular and formal style, it is best to keep to formal shapes. That does not mean that it has to be rectangular; a round pool of irregular shape can still have the 'man-made' look yet make a superb feature. For the elderly or disabled especially, raised ponds can be a great delight.

It is in these situations that fountains can also be particularly effective. In a more natural setting water movement is perhaps best provided by cascades.

In even the smallest garden there is space for something like a bubble fountain, which is little more than a spout of water tumbling over a small group of stones (*see* p. 55). In a heavily paved area this can bring a welcome touch of movement, sound and interest.

If you intend to install fountains or anything that needs a pump, or plan to use lighting (underwater lighting can be enchanting), make arrangements for this before you start construction of the garden. Special cables ought to be laid and protected, and transformers may need to be housed somewhere (although you can use low-voltage equipment with the transformer in house or garage). Go into all this *before* you start laying paving or brickwork!

Do not overlook the possibility of a corner site for a pool in a court-yard type of setting, provided that it is not in constant shade or over-hung by large trees. In this situation a raised, formal pool will look best.

Formal shapes can, of course, be used elsewhere in the garden, especially set in a rectangular lawn, but generally it is the informal shapes that look best among the more natural plantings.

If you are on a sloping site, try to make use of this to produce a natural series of cascades to the pool below. On a flat site it is probably best to avoid cascades (otherwise you will be involved in creating artificial mounds that tend to look very contrived), and settle instead for a *large* informal pool. Always be as generous as you can with size. A larger area of water looks more designed and is usually easier than a small pool to maintain in good balance.

There are many pre-formed pools available, usually made in glass-fibre or moulded plastic. They look large when they are standing upright at a garden centre, but hold comparatively little water, and by the time they are set in the ground and planted they can suddenly seem surprisingly small.

Pond liners are simple to use and they give you more flexibility of design.

If the pool is large enough it can be integrated into the overall design even further by introducing stepping stones (although not straight through the middle unless it is formal in outline). If the garden is large enough, and your skills adequate, you can always introduce a rustic bridge. Be careful with bridges, however; if suddenly discovered as a path is explored they can be enchanting, but stuck pretentiously in full view from all the garden they can look a folly.

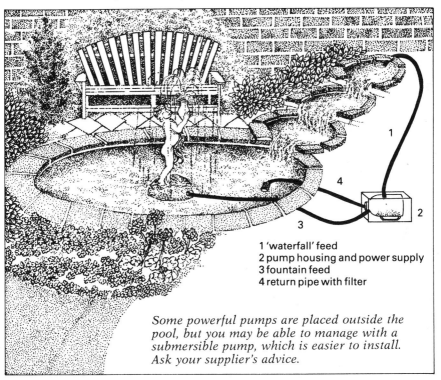

1 'waterfall' feed
2 pump housing and power supply
3 fountain feed
4 return pipe with filter

Some powerful pumps are placed outside the pool, but you may be able to manage with a submersible pump, which is easier to install. Ask your supplier's advice.

Swimming pools are a job for the professional, and in any case can dominate the whole scene unless you are fortunate enough to have a very large garden. Of course if you have more interest in swimming than growing plants this will not matter. If you do want to incorporate a swimming pool, consult a specialist firm as soon as you have an idea of where you would like it. Do not proceed with other aspects of garden construction until you have taken professional advice on this point.

Finally, remember that water looks refreshing on a hot summer's day, and delightful when the water lilies are out and the reeds and irises add height and interest. These will all have gone in winter, and too much expanse of water can then look cold and uninviting. Try to incorporate plants with coloured stems or other interesting features to be reflected in the water to add interest at these times.

Above: An irregular shape is usually better set in a lawn.

Above right: A circular pool in the right setting will give the garden a touch of classic distinction.

Left: A bridge across water has an inevitable charm.

Right: A simple pond, but an effective feature.

Below: A bubble fountain.

13 Summerhouses & Sheds

Although most of us are willing to give careful thought to a summer-house, the garden shed is often dismissed as part of the garden plan. Yet if the summerhouse or the garage are not to become cluttered with garden tools, a shed ought to be given due consideration.

Fortunately it does not matter if it is situated in shade, so it need not take up a prime growing site. That does not mean that it should be tucked away behind trees at the end of the garden; if the children's bicycles and household tools are stored in it, it needs to be readily accessible.

The traditional garden shed has an apex (inverted V) roof with a door at one end. This is still very popular, but there are many designs that

you can consider if the shed has to be in a conspicuous place. In some cases, the borderline between shed and summerhouse is a thin one.

The other major roof shape is the pent type (a single slope, usually from front to back). These can be particularly useful for positioning against a boundary fence or wall, or where you are likely to view it primarily from one angle, rather like a summerhouse.

The positioning of a summerhouse needs very careful thought. If the design is good you will probably want to make it a focal point. Certainly you will need a reasonably open approach to it so that you can sit and admire the garden when you have created it.

If you do not want to look out onto it from the house (or perhaps more importantly, at the house from the summerhouse), try to position it at an angle from the main line of view from the house, perhaps screened by suitable planting.

Aspect is also important. It should provide shelter inside when it is too hot, but be in a sunny situation so that you can enjoy some warmth as well as shelter from the winds on a cold day. If it has a small paved area in front, you will want a sunny position for sunbathing. If you tuck it away underneath trees you will probably have plenty of midges for company.

14 Greenhouses

The days when greenhouses were all of traditional outline, often best tucked away in an inconspicuous place, have long since gone. Apart from the dome-shaped and octagonal (which are nice on a patio, although they do have drawbacks), there are now lean-to and normal apex-roofed kinds available in elegant designs with curved eaves, and coatings that make the aluminium frames less harsh in appearance.

Style and elegance is bought at a price, of course, and if your interest lies more in growing greenhouse crops than making a garden feature of the greenhouse itself, then there is much to be said for the traditional kinds. If you are thinking of buying a greenhouse, much practical advice will be found in a companion volume to this book, *Greenhouses, Cloches and Frames*.

Always try to site the greenhouse where it will receive plenty of sunlight, and avoid the shade of large trees. A lean-to should ideally face south.

The traditional alignment for a greenhouse is north–south, but with aluminium-framed greenhouses, which do not have thick glazing bars, this is not so important. If your main interest lies in raising seedlings in spring, there is much to be said for an east–west alignment, to derive maximum benefit from low-angled sunshine early in the year.

If you intend to use electricity in the greenhouse (useful for so many things, from lights to propagators), or plan to lay on a water supply (useful for some automatic irrigation systems), bear in mind the practical aspects. The further away from the house it is the more costly it will be to lay on these services.

The borderline between some of the modern, even double-glazed, well-styled lean-tos and a conservatory is a blurred one. Positioned over French or patio windows, they blend into almost any design. They make it possible to sit 'outdoors' at almost any time, and help to soften the outline of many buildings when viewed from the garden side.

Decide clearly whether the greenhouse is to be a decorative feature of the garden, or a purely functional structure, in which case the kitchen garden or vegetable plot is a sensible place.

Right, top: A section of the kitchen garden is a popular and sensible place for a conventional greenhouse, provided it is sunny.

Right, below: A greenhouse of more distinctive profile would not look amiss in the flower garden.

15 Unusual Containers

If you happen to have an old horse trough in your garden, you have a ready-made feature that can become a focal point. Most of us have to search round for alternatives.

Although unusual plant containers are most useful and effective for small front gardens or patios, they do have a place in most gardens. Something striking near the front door to greet visitors, or perhaps at the end of the garden to take the eye to a distant point, are other possibilities.

Choice of container needs much thought if it is not to look incongruous. Old baths and lavatories are sometimes used to good effect yet would be totally wrong for a formal setting; an old wooden wheelbarrow planted up with bedding plants can look superb in a cottage garden, but out of place in a modern setting. An old chimney pot planted up with trailing plants, on the other hand, can look right almost anywhere.

Look to your 'junk' with an eye to its potential, but never use anything just for the sake of it. You can always buy large terracotta or glass-fibre containers from garden centres that look very imposing with the right plants, but they are expensive.

An old garden table planted up as an unusual container.

A new — and colourful — life for an old wheelbarrow.

16 Raised Beds

Raised beds are most useful for the disabled or for a retirement garden, but they can also add interest in any garden. In a normal garden they can be introduced naturally at a change of level, perhaps because the site slopes. They also come into their own in a patio setting.

Gardens for the disabled obviously ought to have plenty of raised beds; although as disabilities vary the person concerned should have an important say in their design. It is perfectly feasible to design a whole garden of raised beds, including vegetable beds.

For the elderly who are not disabled, it is worth considering as many raised beds as possible. If borders and beds are raised even by a couple of bricks it will ease the bending.

There is a practical alternative to raising the beds. You can lower the path and create a sunken garden. This usually involves steps, so it is for the able-bodied, but it does perhaps make a more attractive feature.

On a patio, raised beds will add interest as well as height, and provide a useful setting for trailing plants.

Raised beds can make gardening possible for some disabled people, but they should always be consulted about height and width first.

17 Rustic Work & Pergolas

If you want an archway on which to grow plants, you can buy coated metal structures that are easily assembled and erected, with the minimum of fuss. For many of us, however, timber is a more endearing material in the garden (no matter how well archways and pergolas are clothed with plants in summer, they are often fairly naked in winter).

For those whose skills at carpentry do not match their gardening capabilities, it is possible to buy square-section timber pergolas ready for assembly; you only need to provide the holes in the ground and bolt it all together. The handyman gardener will have no difficulty in making his own, as the joints are simple; although for a really strong and imposing structure there is a lot to be said for making brick pillars.

Rustic poles call for even less skill to assemble. A reasonably good eye with the saw and a good supply of strong, long nails are the main requirements.

Pergolas and rustic work can provide valuable height to the scene in a flat garden, but be careful in a small garden where you can overdo it, and it can end up looking like an assortment of scaffolding.

Archways and pergolas nearly always work best when they link one part of the garden with another. Then they have a purpose and do not look too contrived. It is always best to have to walk through them to reach some other feature (if you can equally well skirt round them, there is not a lot of point). If they are the only form of ready access from one part of the garden to another, make sure they are wide enough to walk through with a barrow (when the climbers are in leaf). Remember also to allow sufficient height for cascading plants.

If you want to be ambitious, you can try building a laburnum arch (or one for wisteria). They perhaps look best in a formal garden, but never fail to attract favourable comment that well rewards the early years of training over the metal framework.

Above: A pergola leading to a statue or ornament at the end, backed by shrubs, is a good way to deal with an awkward corner.

Left: A pergola on the grand scale, but there is no reason why the design concept can not be adapted to a small garden, as shown above.

18 Lawns

Lawns are common to most garden designs, regardless of size. There is good reason for this: a nice lawn looks neat and restful, and it sets off the beds and borders superbly.

Sometimes the lawn itself is the main feature of the garden, and that sought-after bowling-green finish is always admired. Such 'show piece' lawns call for much dedicated work, and most gardeners would prefer to spend a greater portion of that time growing flowers.

Usually the lawn is seen as unifying a design, perhaps holding the various elements together, as well as providing a restful area in which to relax (or, if you are young at heart, to play).

Lawns take a lot of maintenance; so bear this in mind when planning. A few simple precautions at this stage can make the whole job easier for years to come.

Serpentine edges are more difficult to maintain neatly, and make mowing a little more difficult. It would be a pity to avoid them as they add so much to a garden, but keep the curves gradual, with wide, gentle sweeps. Avoid abrupt changes of direction and tight curves.

Rectangular lawns are usually best set at an angle across the garden (not right-angles) in a long, narrow plot, to avoid a boring straight-lawns-and-borders approach.

The smaller the garden the more difficult a lawn is to design effectively, and to maintain. A very small lawn looks mean, and there is a high proportion of 'turning' involved when mowing, and a lot of edges to trim in relation to the total area.

In a small, square plot there is not a lot of scope for sweeping curves, and a rectangular lawn would only accentuate the problems of the site. One solution is to make the lawn a circular centrepiece of the garden (*see* page 122).

Generally, the simpler the shape, and larger the expanse, the more effective a lawn becomes; and also simpler to maintain, provided that you have mechanical aids.

If you use a mains-powered mower, bear in mind the amount of cable you have to cope with; sometimes a slight modification to the plan can ease this problem.

Grass seldom grows well under trees. There are woodland grasses that will tolerate shade, but they do not wear as well as ordinary lawn grasses, so try to avoid taking the lawn into these areas.

Narrow strips of grass, perhaps where beds have been allowed to sweep out too far, or where the lawn becomes no more than a path linking two areas, are difficult to mow easily. They also receive a lot of wear, the ground tends to become muddy in wet weather, and bare patches soon appear. It is sometimes better to make one lawn self-contained, have a definite break, possibly with steps or stepping stones linking, and start another separate lawn. There is a lot to be said for having a 'play area' lawn separated and sown with stronger, harder-wearing grasses that will stand up to the punishment that children can mete out.

If the garden is large, areas of rough grass can be quite acceptable, possibly with a narrow path or regularly-cut grass through it if necessary.

There is a lot to be said for rough grass areas in a large garden if you want to keep the labour down. It will only need rough cutting two or three times a year, with a scythe or a suitable mower designed for long grass. Spring-flowering bulbs can be naturalized in these areas with great effect, while wild flowers can be charming in their own right at other times. It is normal to cut some weeks after the spring bulbs have had a chance to die down, then again during August, with perhaps another cut in September.

Non-grass Lawns

Gardeners have always searched for grass substitutes — something with all the merits and none of the drawbacks. Such ideals do not really exist, but there are alternatives if you want to try them in a small area. They will certainly add a touch of interest. Chamomile lawns have always been to the fore among the 'alternatives', and they are pleasant to walk on and fragrant into the bargain. Daisy-like white flowers are produced from mid-summer till autumn with the ordinary kind. Chamomile does not need mowing but the drawback is that it will not stand hard wear like grass.

A 'lawn' of *Sedum acre*, with its bright yellow flowers smothering the succulent green leaves, can be a spectacular sight; plants of this kind are occasionally advertised with wonder claims. Avoid this sedum at all costs: you will save on the mowing, but spend twice as long fighting a losing battle trying to weed it out of the rest of the garden.

19 Garden Furniture

Garden furniture is a contentious point with many gardeners. There can be little doubt that it is useful to have somewhere to sit in the garden. The disagreement arises over whether the furniture should be a feature in its own right or blend inconspicuously into the surroundings.

Deck chairs, hammocks and similar 'mobile' items can be ignored in terms of garden planning. It is those items left out most of the year that need special consideration, for they are a permanent part of the scene.

A wooden garden seat is always worth incorporating, and the two main considerations when siting it should be the view and privacy. Both are usually met if the seat is positioned against the back of the house, looking down the garden, with your back to the house, or if the seat is set at an angle in a bay formed by shrubs. Try to avoid the overhang of trees and shrubs, however, as the drips and leaves are likely to make a mess of the seat, and it will not be a pleasant place to sit.

Sometimes garden furniture alone is enough to enhance a garden.

Cast metal chairs may not be comfortable, but they look right.

Garden seats should be considered at the design stage, to ensure that they blend in unobtrusively.

The courtyard or enclosed patio is different, and often the furniture lends much to the atmosphere. Cast-metal chairs with ornate designs painted white can almost be a decoration in their own right. In many cases it helps to bear the positioning of furniture in mind when planning a small paved area.

Beware of the patio looking like a pavement cafe. Seats built into the patio design overcome this problem. Wood or stone seats are no more uncomfortable to sit on than some cast-metal furniture, and a cushion always helps!

If you are a reasonably competent carpenter, you may be able to build a seat round the bowl of an old tree. This goes against the recommendation of avoiding seats beneath trees, but such a seat has its own special charm.

Garden furniture does not have *to be ornate to look right. It is often much more important to get the positioning right.*

20 Kitchen Garden

Just occasionally the front garden is turned over to vegetables. When everything is growing healthily in early summer the neat rows of various crops can look enticing and even attractive. The problem is that at least part of the ground may be bare and uninteresting at times (especially in winter) so for most of us it is a matter of banishing the vegetable plot to the end of the back garden, where it is out of sight.

Unless one is aiming to produce a model vegetable plot, it is difficult to argue against the 'end of garden' approach, except perhaps on grounds of convenience.

If the garden is large it is not particularly tempting to trek out for a few shoots of sprouting broccoli at the end of the garden on a frosty day. In a wide garden, or one with plenty of land at the side, it is worth trying to incorporate the kitchen garden set off to one side without spoiling the main vista from the house.

Remember that vegetables do not *have* to be grown in long rows. There is nothing wrong with three or four short rows instead of one long one, and you can even grow vegetables perfectly well in 'blocks'. If you bear this in mind, it is sometimes possible to accommodate the vegetables more readily along one side of the garden instead of in a large area at the end.

The herb garden ought to be sited near the kitchen, and because it can make a very decorative feature there is absolutely no reason to banish it to some remote corner.

Tree fruits can be grown in most parts of the garden without detracting from its beauty, but it generally makes sense to keep most fruit and vegetables together in what used to be called a kitchen garden. Fan or espalier trained tree fruits can be particularly decorative, and it is worth considering these as a 'screen' or boundary marker for the kitchen garden, but only if they have a sunny position.

Both fruit and vegetables generally require plenty of sun, but they also appreciate some shelter from cold and drying winds. A hedge along the outer edge is always useful provided that you do not try to grow crops too near it, and there are no large overhanging trees. If you want an internal 'fence', screen block walling can look particularly nice in this situation, and it will also help to filter the wind without causing the damaging currents that can be created by a solid barrier.

Soft fruit will usually benefit from netting, but much depends on where you live. If birds are troublesome and netting is the difference between a full crop and practically none, a fruit cage really is justified. As fruit cages are hardly attractive, however, you may want to bear this in mind when drawing up the plan. In terms of cost, you should be able to make a saving if you can use an existing wall or fence along one side — or even two if the fruit garden is in a corner. The netting can be stretched from the top of the wall or fence over a conventional framework, or even supported temporarily over a few plants by canes (you will need to place an empty yogurt carton over the cane to support the net).

It is usually better to section off the kitchen garden in some way. Dividing up a long, narrow garden in this way will also help avoid a 'ribbon' effect.

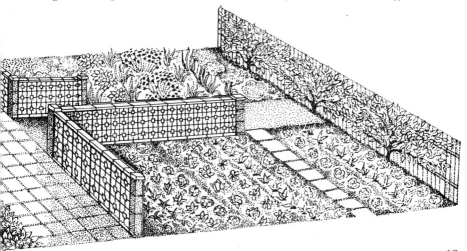

*Two more ideas for integrating the
kitchen garden.*

21 Practical Features

Dustbins and clothes-lines (or driers), compost heaps and incinerators are all part of the garden scene that somehow has to be absorbed with the least visual obtrusion. It is nice to pretend that they do not exist as design problems, but they do.

The clothes-line is always a problem, as it needs a hard path beneath it and the area either side has to be free of anything tall enough for sheets to catch on. This is no easy combination to work into a design, and for that reason the rotary clothes driers are more popular. The area near the back door is often paved anyway, and this provides a suitable site for a rotary drier.

Dustbins also need to be near the house for convenience, but as even 'clean' dustbins can attract flies keep them away from the sitting area. A simple housing on the lines of the illustration (*see* below) looks neat and tidy; you can use the other half for storing other items if you only use one dustbin.

Compost heaps *can* be untidy, smelly things, but they need not be. Proprietary compost bins have the merit of being neat and tidy and for this reason are well worth considering; but a compost heap should be *used*, and if it is at the end of a long garden you are not likely to be putting all the household scraps on regularly. Screen it behind a suitable planting, or even screen block walling if this fits a more formal design better.

22 Children's Garden

It would be a pity to deprive children of the opportunity to play freely in the garden, and, of course, being allowed to play among plants (and better still grow some) may engender a love of gardening as they grow up.

If you want children and a nice garden to co-exist, it is essential to plan your garden with this in mind. First you must allocate a play area. If the children are young it will need to include a sand pit and a surrounding area where the soil can be dug up in play (no amount of sand pits will remove the desire to dig in soil), but for older children a swing, trampoline, or other equipment can simply be placed in a suitable spot out of the main view. For young children, the area should be *in view* from the house, for safety reasons.

It is particularly useful to allocate a portion of the garden as their own, so that they can sow and plant things themselves.

With this combination you are likely to be able to enforce a reasonable 'out of bounds' rule for *your* part of the garden.

Right: Try to get children on your side. Give them their own piece of ground, and encourage them to grow quick and rewarding plants such as bright annuals or vegetables such as lettuces or radishes, which this girl is sowing.

Left: Dustbins are often a problem. You need them near at hand but out of sight. A simple feature like this would be a good project to try if you have not laid bricks before, and it makes a perfectly adequate screen.

23 Lights

Although porch lights are quite popular the full potential of outdoor lighting is seldom appreciated. In the summer months it makes the garden a place to be enjoyed even into the night, and a combination of garden lighting and the fragrance of plants like night-scented stocks (*Matthiola bicornis*) and tobacco plants (nicotiana) makes an enchanting combination on a warm summer's evening.

Even in winter, lighting can add tremendous interest. A spot-light or lanterns illuminating frost or snow on trees and shrubs can be very dramatic.

Remember that you are not trying to illuminate a public building. Keep the lighting subtle and it will be all the more successful. Lanterns are useful placed near steps or other hazards. Floodlights illuminating a tree should be set in a low position, out of sight, and where nobody is likely to walk into the beam.

Illuminated ponds are very attractive, but moving water looks best, especially if the illumination is from underwater lamps. A fountain can almost turn into a rainbow (but do not illuminate the background too, or the effect will be lost).

Above: Moving water is particularly effective.

Left: A porch light is easy to install, and will make a feature of a porch hanging basket even at night.

A Selection of Garden Plants

No book on garden planning can ignore the plants; all the rest is just a setting for them. The difficulty lies in the choice of plants. Even in a large book it is only possible to give a personal selection, whereas in a compact guide like this it is impossible to do more than whet the appetite.

You will often find garden plans that include detailed planting schemes for every border, and often they include uncommon plants you would be hard pressed to find in any but the most specialized nursery. Even then you may not like the plant, or it may not grow well in the soil and situation you can offer. A good portion of the art of good gardening is to plant the subjects that you know will grow and thrive in your conditions.

In the pages that follow you will find the key facts (height, spread, soil requirement and so on) for some of the most desirable garden plants. You should find them readily available from garden centres and nurseries. Plants of a transient nature, such as annuals and biennials, have not been included.

Use these as a shortlist, and add to them as personal preference dictates.

Right: Betula pendula *'Youngii'.*

Broad-leaved Trees

Name	Description	Height and spread
Acer negundo 'Variegatum' (box elder)	Fine foliage tree. Leaves boldly edged yellow.	H: 6 m + (20 ft +) S: 4 m + (13 ft +)
Acer platanoides 'Drummondii'	Strikingly variegated leaves with marginal white band.	H: 10.5 m + (35 ft +) S: 4.5 m + (15 ft +)
Acer pseudoplatanus 'Brilliantissimum'	Charming in spring, when leaves are flushed pink. The colour later changes to pale green.	H: 6 m + (20 ft +) S: 4 m + (13 ft +)
Betula pendula 'Youngii' (weeping birch)	A small weeping tree with dome-shaped head. Silvery bark. Good specimen tree.	H: 6 m + (20 ft +) S: 3 m + (10 ft +)
Catalpa bignonioides 'Aurea'	Very large, pale yellow leaves. Broad habit.	H: 4.5 m + (15 ft +) S: 4.5 m + (15 ft +)
Cotoneaster 'Hybridus Pendulus'	A small evergreen weeping tree, red berries.	H: 1.8 m (6 ft) S: 1.8 m (6 ft)
Eucalyptus gunnii (blue gum)	Young leaves round, older ones sickle-shaped. Blue-green. Evergreen. Quick growth.	H: 15 m + (50 ft +) S: 4 m + (13 ft +)
Laburnum × *watereri* 'Vossii'	Long tassels of yellow flowers in early June. Parts are poisonous.	H: 8 m + (26 ft +) S: 3 m + (10 ft +)
Liquidambar styraciflua (sweet gum)	Maple-like leaves, with rich autumn colour.	H: 6 m + (20 ft +) S: 3.5 m + (12 ft +)
Liriodendron tulipifera (tulip tree)	Strange three-lobed leaves turn yellow in autumn. Greenish tulip-like flowers on mature trees.	H: 11 m + (36 ft +) S: 9 m + (30 ft +)
Magnolia × *soulangiana*	Striking, large pinkish-white flowers in April–May.	H: 6 m (20 ft) S: 4.5 m (15 ft)
Malus floribunda (flowering crab)	Masses of pinkish-white blossom in spring.	H: 3 m + (10 ft +) S: 3 m + (10 ft +)
Malus 'Golden Hornet'	White flowers in May, yellow fruit in autumn.	H: 4.5 m + (15 ft +) S: 3 m + (10 ft +)
Malus 'John Downie'	White flowers in May, conical red-flushed fruit in autumn.	H: 7.5 m + (25 ft +) S: 4.5 m + (15 ft +)
Prunus 'Amanogawa' (flagpole cherry)	Pale pink flowers in April or May. Narrow, upright growth.	H: 4.5 m + (15 ft +) S: 1 m + (3½ ft +)
Prunus 'Kanzan'	Bright pink double flowers in spring. Bold habit.	H: 7.5 m + (25 ft +) S: 6 m + (20 ft +)
Pyrus salicifolia 'Pendula' (willow-leaved pear)	Small tree with weeping habit. Narrow silver-grey leaves.	H: 6 m + (20 ft +) S: 3.5 m + (12 ft +)

Soil and site

Best on well-drained soil. Sun or
partial shade.
Tolerates most soils. Best in sun.

Will grow in any soil. Best in sun
or partial shade.

Will grow on any soil, in sun or
partial shade.

Useful for chalky soil. Not for cold,
windy areas.
Any reasonable soil in full sun.

Best on medium or heavy soil in
full sun.
Avoid very cold areas.
Suitable for all soils, in sun or
partial shade.
Requires an acid soil; avoid chalk
or lime.
Best in full sun.
Will grow in any soil, in sun or
partial shade.

Best on neutral or slightly acid soil
in sheltered site.
Will grow on most soils, in sun or
partial shade.
Tolerates most soils, in sun or
partial shade.
Happy on most soils, in sun or
partial shade.
Best in a well-drained lime-free
soil in full sun.

Prefers well-drained, lime-free
soil, in sun.
Suitable for any fertile soil; best in
sun.
Good town tree.

Liquidambar styraciflua.

Magnolia × soulangiana.

Prunus 'Kanzan'.

79

Broad-leaved Trees continued

Name	Description	Height and spread
Rhus typhina (stag's-horn sumach) *Robinia pseudoacacia* 'Frisia' *Sorbus aria* 'Lutescens' (whitebeam)	Small, spreading tree. Large pinnate leaves colour in autumn. A striking tree with bright yellow leaves, spring to autumn. Leaves creamy white on top in spring, grey-green later.	H: 4.5 m (15 ft) S: 4.5 m (15 ft) H: 6 m + (20 ft +) S: 3 m + (10 ft +) H: 4.5 m + (15 ft +) S: 3 m + (10 ft +)
Sorbus 'Joseph Rock' (mountain ash)	Erect, compact head. Divided leaves colour well in autumn. Sprays of yellow fruits.	H: 4.5 m + (15 ft +) S: 3 m + (10 ft +)

Tall Conifers

Name	Description	Height and spread
Cedrus atlantica 'Glauca' (blue cedar)	Blue-green evergreen foliage. Majestic tree. Good lawn specimen in large garden.	H: 15 m + (50 ft +) S: 4.5 m + (15 ft +)
Chamaecyparis lawsoniana 'Ellwoodii'	Frothy sprays of evergreen grey-green foliage. Columnar.	H: 3 m (10 ft) S: 60 cm (2 ft)
Chamaecyparis nootkatensis 'Pendula'	Weeping evergreen with dramatically cascading branches. Good specimen tree for large garden.	H: 6 m + (20 ft +) S: 1.5 m + (5 ft +)
Cryptomeria japonica 'Elegans'	Blue-green evergreen leaves turn red-bronze in winter.	H: 4.5 m + (15 ft +) S: 3 m + (10 ft +)
Juniperus 'Skyrocket'	A pencil-shaped evergreen with grey-blue foliage.	H: 3.5 m (12 ft) S: 30 cm (1 ft)
Picea pungens 'Hoopsii'	An evergreen of conical habit and glaucous-blue leaves.	H: 7.5 m + (25 ft +) S: 3 m + (10 ft +)
Taxus baccata 'Fastigiata' (Irish yew)	An evergreen of dense, upright growth. There is also a yellow-edged form.	H: 4.5 m + (15 ft +) S: 1.8 m + (6 ft +)

Soil and site
Needs well-drained soil in full sun.
Best in well-drained soil in sun.
Useful on chalk soils in sunny position. Avoid sand. Useful town and seaside tree.
Best on a neutral or acid soil in full sun.

Juniperus *'Skyrocket'*.

Soil and site
Grows in most soils. Needs open site.
Will grow in most soils but best if moist yet drained.
Suitable for most soils. Full sun.
Will thrive in most soils; best in sun. Will grow in most soils, but best in sun. Suitable for most soils, but not shallow or chalky. Will grow on most soils, including chalk, in sun or shade.

Cedrus atlantica *'Glauca'*.

Dwarf Conifers

Name	Description	Height and spread
Chamaecyparis obtusa 'Nana Gracilis'	Dark evergreen foliage held in rounded, curled sprays.	H: 75 cm ($2\frac{1}{2}$ ft) S: 60 cm (2 ft)
Chamaecyparis pisifera 'Boulevard'	Dense silver-blue evergreen foliage. Conical habit.	H: 1.8 m (6 ft) S: 90 cm (3 ft)
Chamaecyparis pisifera 'Filifera Aurea Nana'	Unusual golden, thread-like evergreen foliage. Mop-head.	H: 75 cm ($2\frac{1}{2}$ ft) S: 75 cm ($2\frac{1}{2}$ ft)
Juniperus communis 'Depressa Aurea'	A superb conifer. Bright yellow leaves in spring.	H: 75 cm ($2\frac{1}{2}$ ft) S: 1.2 m (4 ft)
Juniperus × *media* 'Pfitzerana Aurea'	A semi-prostrate evergreen. Leaves yellowish in summer.	H: 1 m ($3\frac{1}{2}$ ft) S: 1.5 m (5 ft)
Juniperus sabina 'Tamariscifolia'	Prostrate evergreen with bluish-green leaves.	H: 38 cm (15 in) S: 1 m ($3\frac{1}{2}$ ft)
Picea glauca 'Albertiana Conica'	Cone-shaped. Bright green evergreen leaves. Slow.	H: 1 m ($3\frac{1}{2}$ ft) S: 60 cm (2 ft)

Climbers

Name	Description	Height and spread
Clematis (large-flowered)	Justifiably popular. Huge flowers. Many kinds.	H: 3 m (10 ft) S: 1.2 m (4 ft)
Clematis montana 'Rubens'	Sheets of smallish pink flowers cover the plant in May.	H: 7.5 m (25 ft) S: 3 m + (10 ft +)
Hedera colchica 'Dentata Variegata' (Persian ivy)	Very large leaves, boldly splashed yellow. Striking.	H: 6 m (20 ft) S: 3 m (10 ft)
Polygonum baldschuanicum (Russian vine)	Very vigorous. Foaming mass of small white flowers July to September. Good for screening.	H: 7.5 m (25 ft) S: 4.5 m (15 ft)
Parthenocissus tricuspidata 'Veitchii' (Boston ivy)	A vigorous self-clinging climber, often mistaken for the Virginia creeper. Rich autumn colour.	H: 9 m (30 ft) S: 3.5 m (12 ft)
Vitis coignetiae	Huge, handsome leaves that colour wonderfully in autumn.	H: 10.5 m (35 ft) S: 6 m (20 ft)
Wisteria floribunda	Magnificent long blue tassels in May and June. Fragrant.	H: 9 m (30 ft) S: 4.5 m (15 ft)

Soil and site

Suitable for most soils. Best in full sun.
Will grow in any reasonable soil, in good light.
Suitable for any good soil; best in sun.
Suitable for any soil, but requires full sun.
Suitable for most soils, but best in full sun.
Will thrive in most soils, in sun or partial shade.
A tough species for most situations, but best in sun.

Juniperus communis *'Depressa Aurea'.*

Picea glauca *'Albertiana Conica'.*

Soil and site

Will grow in most soils, likes lime; sun or semi-shade.

Does well in limy soil; roots in shade, top in sun.
Will thrive almost anywhere, in semi-shade or shade.

Suitable for any soil, including chalk, in semi-shade or shade.

Best in a good loam with unrestricted root run. Succeeds in sun or shade.
Undemanding regarding soil. Sun or shade suits.
Will grow in most soils, but avoid chalk. Needs sun.

Hedera colchica *'Dentata Variegata'.*

Shrubs

Name	Description	Height and spread
Acer palmatum 'Atropurpureum' (Japanese maple)	Attractively lobed, bronzy-crimson leaves.	H: 4.5 m (15 ft) S: 3.5 m (12 ft)
Amelanchier lamarckii (Snowy mespilus)	Masses of small white flowers in April. Autumn colour.	H: 3.5 m (12 ft) S: 3 m (10 ft)
Azaleas (various)	These invaluable spring flowers come in many varied forms.	H: 0.6-2.1 m (2-7 ft) S: 0.6-1.8 m (2-6 ft)
Buddleia davidii (butterfly bush)	Arching sprays of bold flowers (mainly blues and purples), July to Oct.	H: 2.4 m (8 ft) S: 2.4 m (8 ft)
Camellia × williamsii 'Donation'	Large, semi-double pink flowers, March to May. Hardy.	H: 1.8 m (6 ft) S: 1.8 m (6 ft)
Cornus stolonifera 'Flaviramea'	Useful because the yellowish-green stems add interest in winter.	H: 1.8 m (6 ft) S: 1.8 m (6 ft)
Cortaderia selloana 'Pumila' (Pampas grass)	Popular evergreen grass, silvery flower 'plumes'.	H: 1.2 m (4 ft) S: 90 cm (3 ft)
Cytisus × praecox (Warminster broom)	Spectacular mass of creamy-yellow flowers in May.	H: 1.5 m (5 ft) S: 1.5 m (5 ft)
Elaeagnus pungens 'Maculata' (wood olive)	Evergreen leaves strikingly splashed with yellow. Useful in winter.	H: 2.4 m (8 ft) S: 2.4 m (8 ft)
Euonymus fortunei radicans 'Emerald 'n' Gold'	Green and gold leaves. Trailing or climbing habit. Evergreen.	H: 30 cm (1 ft) S: 45 cm (1½ ft)
Fatsia japonica	Large, hand-like leaves. Globular white flower heads, October. Evergreen.	H: 2.1 m (7 ft) S: 1.5 m (5 ft)
Garrya elliptica	Evergreen with magnificent catkins in January-February.	H: 1.8 m (6 ft) S: 1.5 m (5 ft)
Genista lydia	Cascading masses of golden flowers in May and June.	H: 45 cm (1½ ft) S: 45 cm (1½ ft)
Hamamelis mollis 'Pallida' (witch hazel)	Fragrant yellow flowers on bare stems. December-March. Yellow autumn colour.	H: 3 m (10 ft) S: 2.4 m (8 ft)
Pieris formosa 'Forrestii'	White flowers in April and May. Young shoots/leaves red. Evergreen.	H: 2.4 m (8 ft) S: 2.4 m (8 ft)

Soil and site

Best in neutral or acid soil, sheltered from cold winds. Sun or semi-shade.
Will grow in most soils, in sun or partial shade.
All require acid, peaty soil, and partial shade.
Will grow in any reasonable soil, even limy, but needs full sun.

Best in a peaty soil, in partial shade.
Best in a moist soil in sun or partial shade.

Best in light soil or medium loam in full sun.

Best on well-drained soil in full sun.
Any soil except shallow chalk. Sun or shade.

Will grow in any soil, including chalk, in sun or shade.

Needs light or medium soil in partial shade. Not hardy in cold areas.
Best in well-drained soil. Sun or shade. Not hardy in cold districts.

Best in light acid or neutral soil in full sun.
Best in moist loam with added peat. Suitable for sun or semi-shade. Shelter.

Needs, peaty, acid soil in sun. Not totally hardy in cold areas.

Azalea *'Hinomayo'*.

Cytisus × praecox.

Genista lydia.

85

Shrubs continued

Name	Description	Height and spread
Potentilla (shrubby type)	There are many forms of this long-flowering (May–October) shrub. Mainly in shades of yellow.	H: 0.3–1.2 m (1–4 ft) S: 1–1.2 m ($3\frac{1}{2}$–4 ft)
Salvia officinalis 'Purpurascens' (purple-leaf sage)	A useful foliage shrub. Stems and young leaves suffused purple. Evergreen.	H: 60 cm (2 ft) S: 60 cm (2 ft)
Senecio greyi	Felted, grey-white leaves. Yellow flowers June–July.	H: 90 cm (3 ft) S: 90 cm (3 ft)
Spiraea × *bumalda* 'Goldflame'	A dwarf shrub with young growth flushed gold. Red flowers.	H: 75 cm ($2\frac{1}{2}$ ft) S: 75 cm ($2\frac{1}{2}$ ft)
Weigela florida 'Variegata'	Leaves edged creamy-white. Pink flowers in June.	H: 1.2 m (4 ft) S: 1.2 m (4 ft)
Yucca filamentosa	Evergreen with bold, spiky leaves. White flowers July–August.	H: 75 cm ($2\frac{1}{2}$ ft) S: 90 cm (3 ft)

Herbaceous Border Plants

Name	Description	Height and spread
Acanthus spinosus (bear's breeches)	Bold spikes of mauve-purple flowers, July–September.	H: 1.2 m (4 ft) S: 60 cm (2 ft)
Achillea 'Gold Plate' (yarrow)	Flat yellow flower heads, June–Sept. Ferny foliage.	H: 1.5 m (5 ft) S: 75 cm ($2\frac{1}{2}$ ft)
Alchemilla mollis (lady's mantle)	Feathery sprays of yellow flowers, June–August.	H: 45 cm ($1\frac{1}{2}$ ft) S: 30 cm (1 ft)
Aster novi-belgii (Michaelmas daisy)	Popular late border plants. Daisy-like heads September–October.	H: 30–75 cm (1–$2\frac{1}{2}$ ft) S: 30–45 cm (1–$1\frac{1}{2}$ ft)
Astilbe × *arendsii*	Feathery flower plumes, several colours, June–August.	H: 60–90 cm (2–3 ft) S: 45–60 cm ($1\frac{1}{2}$–2 ft)
Echinops ritro (globe thistle)	Grey-green leaves, steel-blue globular flower heads, July–August.	H: 1 m ($3\frac{1}{2}$ ft) S: 60 cm (2 ft)
Euphorbia polychroma (spurge)	Mound of bright yellow bracts, April–May.	H: 45 cm ($1\frac{1}{2}$ ft) S: 30 cm (1 ft)

Soil and site	
Will thrive in most soils, in sun or partial shade.	
Best in a light or medium soil in full sun.	
Best in well-drained soil in full sun.	Weigela florida *'Variegata'*.

Will thrive in most soils, in sun or partial shade.

Best in a light or medium soil in full sun.

Best in well-drained soil in full sun.
Suitable for any soil, in sun or shade.
Will grow in any soil, in sun or shade.
Light or medium soil in full sun.
Not fully hardy in cold areas.

Weigela florida *'Variegata'*.

Alchemilla mollis.

Soil and site

Needs moisture-retentive soil, sun or semi-shade.
Best on light, chalky soils, in full sun.

Suits most soils, in sun or partial shade.
Best on fertile, fairly moist soil in sun.

Moist soil is essential. Sun or partial shade.
Any reasonable soil suitable, in full sun.

Best in well-drained soil in sun or partial shade.

Euphorbia polychroma.

87

Herbaceous Border Plants continued

Name	Description	Height and spread
Geranium 'Johnson's Blue'	Dished, bright blue flowers, May–August.	H: 30 cm (1 ft) S: 30 cm (1 ft)
Helleborus niger (Christmas rose)	Saucer-shaped, usually white, flowers, December–March.	H: 30 cm (1 ft) S: 30 cm (1 ft)
Hosta fortunei 'Albopicta' (plantain lily)	Creamy yellow young leaves, margined green. Striking.	H: 60 cm (2 ft) S: 45 cm ($1\frac{1}{2}$ ft)
Ligularia clivorum 'Desdemona'	Large vivid orange flowers, July–September; purplish leaves.	H: 1.2 m (4 ft) S: 60 cm (2 ft)
Lupinus 'Russell Hybrids'	Magnificent spikes in self and bi-colours, June.	H: 90 cm (3 ft) S: 45 cm ($1\frac{1}{2}$ ft)
Monarda didyma (bergamot)	Distinctive, tufted, mainly pink or red flowers clear of leaves, July–August.	H: 90 cm (3 ft) S: 45 cm ($1\frac{1}{2}$ ft)
Nepeta mussinii (catmint)	Aromatic grey-green leaves.	H: 30 cm (1 ft) S: 30 cm (1 ft)
Oenothera missouriensis (evening primrose)	Large, saucer-shaped bright yellow flowers, June–September.	H: 25 cm (10 in) S: 30 cm (1 ft)
Paeonia (peony)	Huge, globular, double or single flowers in various colours.	H: 75-90 cm ($2\frac{1}{2}$-3 ft) S: 45-60 cm ($1\frac{1}{2}$-2 ft)
Phlox paniculata	Bold, bright flower head in various colours, July–September.	H: 75-90 cm ($2\frac{1}{2}$-3 ft) S: 30-38 cm (12-15 in)
Phormium tenax (New Zealand flax)	Imposing plants with large, strap-like leaves. Various colour forms.	H: 45-100 cm ($1\frac{1}{2}$-$3\frac{1}{2}$ ft) S: 45-90 cm ($1\frac{1}{2}$-3 ft)
Salvia superba 'East Friesland'	Spikes of violet-purple flowers, July–September.	H: 45 cm ($1\frac{1}{2}$ ft) S: 45 cm ($1\frac{1}{2}$ ft)
Sedum spectabile 'Autumn Joy'	Flat heads of salmon-pink flowers, August–October. Succulent leaves.	H: 60 cm (2 ft) S: 30 cm (1 ft)

Ground Cover Plants

Name	Description	Height and spread
Ajuga reptans 'Burgundy Glow' (bugle)	Rose and magenta leaves edged grey and white. Blue flowers in May and June.	H: 10 cm (4 in) S: 30 cm (1 ft)
Bergenia cordifolia (elephant's ears)	Large leaves retained through winter. Flowers, usually pink, April–May.	H: 25 cm (10 in) S: 30 cm (1 ft)

Prefers well-drained soil in sun or
partial shade.
Best in fairly moist soil, in partial
or full shade.
Best in a moist soil, in partial or
full shade.

Needs a moist soil in full sun.

Best in light soil in sun or partial
shade.
Best in moist soil, in sun or partial
shade.

Prefers well-drained soil in full
sun.
Very useful for light, dry slopes in
full sun.
Needs a moist, rich soil, in sun or
partial shade.
Medium to heavy, moist soil, sun
or semi-shade.
Rich moist soil in sun or partial
shade. Best for mild areas.

Will grow in most soils, but
provide full sun.
Easily grown in ordinary soil in
full sun.

Lupins, 'Russell Hybrids'.

Hosta fortunei *'Albopicta'.*

Soil and site

Will grow in most soils, in sun or
shade, although best if moist, in
sun.
Happy in most soils, in sun or
partial shade.

Phormium tenax *'Variegatum'.*

Ground Cover Plants continued

Name	Description	Height and spread
Erica carnea (heath)	Most varieties covered with white, pink or red flowers in winter or spring.	H: 25 cm (10 in) S: 30-60 cm (1-2 ft)
Geranium endressii	Masses of pink conspicuous flowers, June–September.	H: 45 cm (1½ ft) S: 30 cm (1 ft)
Hypericum calycinum (rose of Sharon)	Large, pale yellow flowers. Evergreen. Invasive.	H: 30 cm (1 ft) S: widely spreading
Lamium maculatum 'Beacon Silver'	Silvery leaves. Rose-pink flowers, May–June.	H: 10 cm (4 in) S: 25 cm (10 in)
Pachysandra terminalis 'Variegata'	White and green evergreen leaves. Not invasive.	H: 15 cm (6 in) S: 60 cm (2 ft)
Polygonum affine	Good carpeter with small, pink, poker-like spikes, June–September.	H: 25 cm (10 in) S: 45 cm (1½ ft)
Stachys lanata (lambs' ears)	Silvery, 'woolly' leaves. Pinkish flowers, July.	H: 30 cm (1 ft) S: 60 cm (2 ft)
Thymus serpyllum (thyme)	Many kinds, some variegated. Evergreen, aromatic leaves.	H: 5 cm (2 in) S: 60 cm (2 ft)
Vinca major 'Variegata'	Evergreen leaves margined creamy-white. Blue flowers.	H: 23 cm (9 in) S: 90 cm (3 ft)

Plants for Cracks in Paving

Name	Description	Height and spread
Acaena microphylla	Moss-like greeny-bronze leaves; crimson burs in summer.	H: 5 cm (2 in) S: 45 cm (1½ ft)
Achillea 'King Edward'	Rosettes of feathery grey-green foliage. Yellow flowers.	H: 20 cm (8 in) S: 15 cm (6 in)
Armeria maritima (thrift)	Tufts of grass-like leaves and pink or red flowers, May–July.	H: 15 cm (6 in) S: 25 cm (10 in)
Campanula carpatica	Saucer-shaped flowers, white to blue shades, June–August.	H: 25 cm (10 in) S: 30 cm (1 ft)
Campanula cochleariifolia	Dainty, blue or white flowers on wiry stems, June–September.	H: 10 cm (4 in) S: 30 cm (1 ft)
Dianthus deltoides (maiden pink)	White, pink or red flowers; June–July. Narrow grey leaves.	H: 15 cm (6 in) S: 10 cm (4 in)
Thymus serpyllum (thyme)	Aromatic leaves. Mat-forming. Various kinds, some variegated.	H: 5 cm (2 in) S: 60 cm (2 ft)

Soil and site
Will grow in most light or medium soils, but appreciates peat. Sun.
Will grow in most soils, in sun or partial shade.
Prefers a light or medium soil. Sun or shade.
Suits most soils; best in partial shade.
Best in moist soil in shade. Avoid chalk.
Will grow in most soils, in sun or partial shade.
Best on well-drained soil, in full sun, but adaptable.
Prefers light or medium, chalky soil in full sun.
Will grow in most soils, in sun or shade.

Polygonum affine.

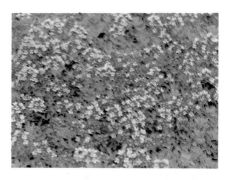

Thymus *'Bressingham Seedling'.*

Soil and site
Best with good drainage and full sun.
Will grow in most soils, in full sun.
Ordinary well-drained soil in full sun.
Best in well-drained soil with some lime. Full sun.
Best in moist but well-drained site. Full sun.
Light or medium, chalky soil, in full sun.
Prefers light or medium, chalky soil in full sun.

Armeria maritima.

Ideas to Follow

Most of this book so far has been about the principles of garden design, about techniques, about the building blocks of design that will help you to construct a more interesting garden. It has deliberately avoided presenting you with set plans, which are extremely unlikely to be the solution to *your* particular problem, even if by some good fortune one of them happened to fit the size and shape of your garden. A highly detailed planting scheme is also likely to cost you a fair sum of money to implement if it does not happen to use a fair proportion of the plants you already have in your garden. In addition, one person's choice of plants is unlikely to correspond exactly with another's.

It is comparatively easy to teach most people the basic rules of sentence construction, and to show someone how to check their spelling in a dictionary. It is no small step from there to writing a good novel. It is the same with creating a garden, and sometimes just as much 'rewriting' is necessary if you do not quite get things right. What matters is ideas (good ideas) and no-one has a monopoly on these. In creating your garden it may be best to take what you like that other people have done, and to try to work these features into your own plan. Perhaps you can modify them and improve on them. It is probably better to do this than to try to be original in everything that you do.

You will also find that looking at what other people have done overcomes that awful sinking feeling that comes when you are confronted with your sheet of blank paper and you have to be creative and put something down.

The next 33 pages of the book are devoted not to detailed garden plans but to ideas that other gardeners have tried and found to work. Someone else's solution to a particular design problem may spark off an idea that provides a solution for your own problem.

If you 'mix and merge' the features that you like, there is no reason why you should not end up with a personally designed garden that is full of good ideas, and that will suit your individual taste, which is what really matters most in the end.

It is not size alone that makes a successful garden, but the careful selection of plants and an ability to create a setting to match.

Beds for Specimen Trees and Shrubs

A bed to take a single specimen tree can be a problem. Nothing much will grow in it once the tree is anything more than a sapling, and in any case such beds tend to be too small to make any kind of a display. You can replace the grass you removed when planting and let the lawn go right up to the trunk. Unfortunately as each year passes mowing round the tree becomes increasingly difficult, and there is always the danger of damaging the bark with the mower. You will also find that the grass will never do well, even if you resow with shade-tolerant grasses. The grass is also likely to compete with the tree for nutrients during the early years.

Generally it is best to make a small bed for the tree if you can, but try to make it as interesting as possible. These pictures show two ways that gardeners have overcome this problem.

Fig. 1 shows how the bed has been raised slightly with rocks, and then filled with a peat mulch. This has made what could be an uninteresting section of the garden while the tree is still young into a feature in its own right. It is also giving the young tree the best chance of establishment.

Fig. 1

Fig. 2

Fig. 2 shows an interesting way in which the bed has been enlarged as the tree has grown, although at first sight it appears to have been constructed at one time. There is a small raised bed in the centre, and the area was enlarged by setting cobbles around it; this makes it easy to continue enlarging in stages. Finally a row of bricks has been added around the edge to extend the bed and give it its neat finish. Had the bed been as large as this initially the young tree would have looked lost, and if the bed had not been enlarged mowing would have been almost impossible even if the grass had grown.

This picture also demonstrates the importance of careful choice of trees for small gardens. This *Cupressus macrocarpa* 'Lutea' is really a very large conifer. When the owner realized his mistake he decided to clip it fairly hard each year, treating it rather like a hedge, and by doing so has managed to turn the mistake into an attractive centre-piece for his garden.

Low-maintenance Gardens

The two pictures on this page show how low-maintenance need not necessarily mean low interest gardens. Both have plenty of impact yet need the minimum of attention.

Fig. 3 shows that a small open-plan garden need not necessarily be little more than grass with a few shrubs. The area has been paved in an irregular pattern to avoid it looking too harsh and dominating the low-growing plants, and dwarf conifers and heathers chosen to hold the main interest. Apart from annually clipping over the heathers, this garden will need virtually no looking after. Interest is held by the shape and colour of the conifers.

In Fig. 4 the small front garden of a retirement bungalow has been cleverly designed and planted to provide plenty of interest yet take hardly any looking after. Again heathers and conifers have been used. In this case pebbles from the beach have been set in concrete to avoid the need to weed among the plants.

Fig. 3

Fig. 4

Archways and Arbours

The two pictures on this page are very different in scale, but they both show how well some form of archway can hold a garden together and create a sense of adventure. Whether it is a long pergola on the grand scale, like the one on p. 62 or the metal archway in Fig. 5, there is an impression of somewhere to explore, and in the garden shown on p. 62 it avoids a long, narrow plot appearing to be split in half by the path along the centre.

A laburnum arch is particularly spectacular. Unfortunately it requires a large space, as you need a long stretch to create a 'tunnel' of golden tassels (*see* Fig. 6). You also need a strong iron framework, high enough to allow you to walk beneath the cascades of flowers when the plants are in bloom. Because you also need time to train them and will have to wait a few years for them to flower, this idea is really a long-term project where you intend to stay in the same house for a long time, so that you can benefit from your labours when it comes into its full glory.

Fig. 5

Fig. 6

A Roof Garden

A roof garden can look very attractive, as Fig. 7 shows, but it needs careful thought. All your designs are going to be restricted by structural considerations, and for that reason they have not been considered at length in this book. You really should seek professional advice before you start putting paving, compost and even water on your roof.

This 'roof garden' was designed by students from a horticultural college for the Chelsea Flower Show in 1982, and although on *terra firma* could be constructed on a roof.

The most surprising element of this garden is the pool. Before you go putting vast amounts of water on your roof, however, it should be pointed out that the actual depth of this one is about 8 cm (3 in), but the black liner gives it an impression of much greater depth.

Always use a lightweight compost for beds and containers on roof-tops and balconies.

A Touch of Elegance

You do not need a large area to create a sense of quality and elegance, but you do usually need money. However you could concentrate on just a small area and indulge yourself with something a little expensive, even if you do not make the rest of the garden to the same standard.

It is interesting that water plays an important role in all four of the gardens illustrated opposite. The area need not be large, and in Fig. 8 it is no more than a fountain in a corner of the garden. In garden construction terms the cost of this would be quite high per square metre for materials, but bear in mind that in this instance little else is costly, and it has transformed what would otherwise be a very dull small lawn into something a little special.

The pool shown in Fig. 9 is no more than a rectangular pool, but the restrained fountain and the setting transform it into a very classical piece of design. The same pool outside the French windows of a modern estate-type house would probably look very different. It is the way elements are integrated that produce the designed effect; copying a single feature or idea will not in itself produce results. Here it is a combination of containers, seats, mosaic tiled floor, and the decorated wall in the covered sitting area that give this scene a touch of classic elegance.

Fig. 10 shows what could be created in a garden of quite modest size. A garden like this is high on hard landscaping and low on soft landscaping (plants). If plants are your main interest you could find this

Fig. 7

Fig. 8

Fig. 9

Fig. 10

frustrating, but if you want a garden of charm and elegance, and you can afford to construct a garden like this (remember that you can tackle it in stages over quite a long period if you want to spread the labour and the cost) then you will have a garden that is sure to be admired. This one was built for *Ideal Home* magazine for the Chelsea Flower Show in 1982, by David Stevens.

The garden in Fig. 11, also designed for the 1982 Chelsea Show, shows a simple, open design suitable for a modest-sized rectangular garden. This is not a plantsman's garden, but is just right if you want to sit and enjoy your garden rather than spend a lot of time working in it. This design shows the important role of statuary in creating a focal point as well as adding a special touch of elegance.

Brighter Boundaries

Some of the brightest boundaries are flowering hedges (*see* pp. 40-3). but hedges are not always appropriate (as Fig. 12 shows, sometimes a retaining wall is necessary because of the site), and not everyone wants hedges, because they represent too much work, they can take up too much growing space, or simply because they do not like the appearance.

Fig. 12 shows how a very functional brick retaining wall, that could look very boring, has been made quite attractive by raising the ground a little more above it and creating a rock garden so that the flow of plants tumbles towards the edge, with cascading plants such a *Alyssum saxatile* softening the edge of the wall. Because it also brings the rock plants closer to eye level, they can be appreciated by passers-by.

The approach in Fig. 13 has been to merge the inside of the garden with the outside to mask the formal boundary. Shrubs still provide some privacy but the small 'rock bank' on the roadside manages to avoid the formality of either hedge, wall or fence. It is also a bonus for passers-by.

Fig. 14 shows a garden boundary designed for the passer-by's benefit: the bed is not visible from the garden itself, and the hedge behind it still needs to be maintained (a chore you may be prepared to accept for the privacy it gives). If there were more displays like this along the roadside our journeys would be much brighter.

A Sense of Anticipation

It is always a good idea to introduce an element of surprise, a sense of anticipation, into your design. The pictures on pp. 102-3 show how

Fig. 11

Fig. 12

Fig. 13

Fig. 14

various gardeners have achieved this by carefully positioning shrub and flower beds in the lawn.

Fig. 15 shows how it can be done effectively in a large garden, with large beds of tall-growing shrubs dividing up sections of grass. You can achieve the same effect on a much smaller scale too. Fig. 16 is a garden of medium size, but the way the entrance to the garden from the house end has been angled, so that you approach it almost sideways with the lawn stretching off right and left, makes the garden look much bigger than it is. The front of the house is just to the right, and to the left the lawn sweeps down to the road and more surprises. Fig. 17 shows the road end of the garden. Although only a few metres from the road, the screening of trees and shrubs and the grass path leading through them off to the left manage to give not only an impression of greater size but also a sense of anticipation of more to come. You feel you have to go down the path to see what is there even if it does only bring you out onto the road around the next shrub.

The same principle has been employed in the design of the garden in Fig. 18. This long, narrow garden has been designed with large sweeping bays on the right and island beds on the left to channel the eye into a sense of direction. Each bay on the right contains its own surprises in the form of interesting plants and plantings, and in one of them there is even a play area for the children, including a large trampoline — all of which is hidden from view.

In all of these examples the effect was not instant. There is no short cut that will make the plants grow large enough to form a screen more quickly, but unless you plan your garden for a few years ahead, time itself will not create an interesting garden.

Fig. 15

Fig. 16

Fig. 17   Fig. 18

Town Gardens

If you live in an area of rolling countryside, or if you are surrounded
by other well-designed gardens with no background to detract the eye,
or even if you have a large enough garden to create your own little bit
of perfection, you start with a tremendous advantage. In so many
gardens the background is obtrusive (even ugly) and often the area you
can 'landscape' is small.

The pictures on p. 104 show you what can be done even on the most
unpromising sites.

Even if you look out onto a factory wall, there is much that can be
done to create an oasis of interest and colour (*see* Fig. 19). To prevent
the walls dominating the scene, a framework of timber has been used
to provide support for a magnificent hanging display. The paved area
avoids distracting from the display, which depends heavily on bedding
plants, and is somewhere to sit with your back to the walls so that you
can enjoy the rest of the garden, which even includes a small pond.

The garden in Fig. 20 shows what can be done in a small town garden
(this one was designed by Geoff and Faith Whiten for the 1982 Chelsea
Flower Show). By retaining some areas of grass and by allowing
reasonable planting areas between the paving, it has been possible to
avoid an over-paved feeling. It is very much a garden to sit in.

The garden in Fig. 21 is an awkward small corner plot with little scope for design. The drawbacks have been overcome here by concentrating on a quality 'bowling green' lawn with a few small beds that depend heavily on bedding plants for colour and interest. The planted wheelbarrow in the porch shows how vital planted containers can be; this feature does much to hold the garden together. In effect the lawn has become a setting for displaying bedding plants effectively. Remember, however, that a poorly-maintained, coarse lawn could detract from this sort of effect.

Fig. 19 *Fig. 20*

Fig. 21

Bright Bedding

If you want to avoid a lot of work, and possibly expense, beds that require replanting perhaps twice a year with bedding plants are best omitted. They can also look totally out of place in an informal garden, whereas on a very small scale in a tiny garden they can look mean and unnatural (particularly narrow 'ribbon' beds).

That is the negative side of bedding. If you can afford the time to look after the beds, and are prepared to make a real feature of them, they can be one of the brightest elements in the garden.

To use annuals effectively, make the beds as wide and as large as possible so that you can plant in large drifts or sweeps, rather than dotting the plants about trying to make some intricate pattern. The illustrations on these two pages show both summer and spring bedding, and you should be prepared to replant with one as soon as the other has finished; bare soil does not make an attractive feature and spring bedding can be particularly welcome after the dull days of winter.

If you have a small garden with little scope for an elaborate garden design, and you do not fancy paving, there is much to be said for making bedding the main feature, so that you always have bold splashes of colour to make a real impact. Fig. 22 shows how interesting spring bedding can be even in a small garden. The hyacinths are interplanted with tulips and polyanthuses. Even a small area like this can require many bulbs, however, and it can be a costly scheme to maintain.

You can keep the cost down by raising plants like polyanthuses and wallflowers from seed.

Fig. 22

Fig. 23

Summer bedding in particular benefits from bold drifts (Fig. 23). Although schemes are often designed around island beds, they are often particularly effective against a background such as a wall provided that the bed is large enough. Even an odd corner of the garden that you have earmarked for later planting with more permanent subjects can be turned into a colourful feature in the meantime with annuals.

Island Beds

You do not have to have a large garden to use island beds effectively. Even small islands can be impressive if they are in proportion to the rest of the garden, are well planted, and above all carefully positioned. The island bed in Fig. 24 shows how impressive even a small island can be if planted with thought. The way the bed has been positioned within the garden avoids it looking as contrived as it would if positioned more centrally, and the lawn leading away behind them adds interest to what would otherwise be a rather uninteresting corner of the garden.

Island rock beds are tempting, but they really need to be large to look designed (they will never look as natural as a rock garden on a naturally sloping site, but the majority of gardens are on fairly level ground, so a compromise may be the only solution). The recently planted island rock bed in Fig. 26 is about the minimum size that will produce an effective design. Fig. 25 shows how it can work if the bed is large enough.

Fig. 24

Fig. 25

Fig. 26

Fig. 27

Fig. 28

Stones and Gravel

Gravel is a very 'sympathetic' material in the garden. It blends surprisingly well with plants, and it provides a change of texture from grass and paving. It is used quite often for large driveways, but it can be used much more creatively. There is no reason why you cannot make a 'gravel garden'. Fig. 27 shows a very individual garden where the whole area has been gravelled and the plants arranged in a very informal way with meandering paths between them. Another design by the same gardener (Fig. 28) shows the imaginative use of stones and gravel to create a 'dried river bed'. Schemes like these make interesting features and the plants are often displayed very effectively.

If you have a large garden, gravel paths can look particularly natural, especially if low-growing plants can cascade over the edges.

Even on a small scale it is worth thinking about a gravelled area as part of the design. Fig. 29 shows how a feature can be made of it.

Fig. 29

Fig. 30

Fig. 31

Fig. 32

Small Beds

Sometimes even a very small bed can add interest, so do not feel that small necessarily means fussy or uninteresting. The tiny bed in Fig. 30 is only large enough for one small shrub and carpeting plants around the edge, but by placing it in a key position it takes on an importance much beyond its size, and has become a focal point in the design.

A very small bed, like this one at the edge of a patio (Fig. 31), can be made more interesting by choosing suitable plants.

The idea of a single plant in a small bed can be extended to larger shrubs or small trees. As Fig. 32 shows, they break up what could otherwise be a flat boring view, adding both height and interest.

Letting Plants Predominate

Sometimes it is possible to create a superb garden that looks so natural that it may appear unplanned. The photograph (Fig. 33) of a fairly small walled garden show just how effectively the plants have been allowed to predominate. There is very little hard landscaping; the success of the garden lies in the careful choice of plants, which give the scene height, shape and texture.

Although a garden like this may look as though it just 'happened', it is perhaps more difficult to create than one with more hard landscaping. The choice of summerhouse and garden ornament have to be made with care and taste if the scene is not to be marred.

A garden like this shows the importance of choosing just a few trees or shrubs wisely. The Japanese maple with its interesting shape and yellow foliage dominates the garden when it is in leaf. A less impressive tree would not have the same impact, and it shows the importance of the actual plants when you are designing a garden.

Fig. 33

Using Climbers

Climbers seldom appear on the outline garden plan, as features are rarely designed around them. Nevertheless when it comes to compiling a planting list they should be high on the priorities. They can transform an uninteresting aspect of the garden (an old shed, a brick wall, perhaps an old tree-stump) into something quite attractive. They can be used to disguise or to beautify.

Climbers can also be used to enhance the house. Climbing roses against a white cottage wall present the timeless feeling of a real cottage garden (Fig. 34). Climbing roses are even an attractive feature

Fig. 34

Fig. 35

Fig. 36

Fig. 37

against the setting of a more modern home (Fig. 35).

If you have a large brick wall to cover and you do not mind it being bare in the winter, a plant like *Parthenocissus tricuspidata* is self-clinging and will cover it well with green leaves during the summer. It will provide a really spectacular (albeit fairly short-lived) sight in autumn when the leaves take on their autumn colour (Fig. 36).

One of the most useful climbers for covering an unsightly object, such as an oil tank or possibly an old garden shed, is the Russian vine (*Polygonum baldschuanicum*).

Climbers should not be looked upon purely as camouflage, however. Some are so spectacular in flower that they can become one of the key features in the garden. Wisterias fall into this category (Fig. 37).

A Wild Garden

If you have a large garden but neither the time nor resources to keep it well maintained, it is best to design it so that you can keep some parts that need more care well-maintained, and let the 'wilder' areas look after themselves to some extent. Fig. 38 shows how sections of the lawn have been left uncut for much longer periods than the main lawn. In a rural setting this can blend in well with the landscape, and the wild flowers that grow in the uncut grass bring colour and a charm of their own. In this garden wild orchids grow among the grass, and pockets of interest are created for most of the summer.

Creating areas of 'wild' garden can do more than cut down on labour. It can stimulate an interest in the wildlife that it attracts, and the real beauty of many of our wild flowers can be appreciated if you do not feel obliged to regard them all as unwanted weeds to be pulled up on first sight.

Fig. 38

Gardening Without Bending

There are many gardeners whose physical abilities do not match their enthusiasm. Not only is it frustrating for those confined to wheelchairs, but age can also take its toll and make bending and lifting increasingly difficult. That is no reason for not being able to enjoy gardening, however, and careful design can do much to make the hobby more enjoyable for those with restricted physical abilities.

If you are disabled in some way yourself, you know what you can and cannot do, so you will soon see the limitations of some ideas; if you are designing the garden for someone else, consult them about your ideas first. The beds may be too wide to reach over, for instance, and the height of a raised bed might vary depending on whether you are likely to be working on it standing or from a wheelchair.

One of the finest examples of a garden designed for the disabled is the model garden at the Royal Horticultural Society's garden at Wisley in Surrey (Fig. 39). This shows how even ponds and vegetables can be accommodated in raised beds. A garden like this is quite costly to build, but the running costs are low, and not much work is needed to keep it in good condition. Digging is not such a problem, as there is no soil compaction from trampling feet. You can, in effect, practise the 'four-foot bed' system of no digging (this works on the principle of digging not being necessary because the soil is not compacted if you can reach all parts from paths either side).

Fig. 39

If you want low-maintenance raised beds you can plant suitable shrubs. If the prospect of too much brickwork deters you, it is always possible to plant trailers, such as ivy (Fig. 40) to cascade over the side and soften the appearance.

If you are a 'handy' person, you can make a raised bed into an attractive feature in its own right. The bed of hyacinths (Fig. 41) has been made from local flints concreted together. One of the advantages of raised beds is that fragrant plants, such as hyacinths, can be appreciated even more than usual.

Fig. 40   *Fig. 41*

Making Use of Containers

You may think that containers are something that one adds to the garden after the design stage — fillers that brighten up odd gaps. They are useful for that, but if you regard them rather like garden ornaments then they can take on a more important role. In Fig. 42 for instance an area has been set aside for a group of containers to make a special feature. In the small front garden on a corner site shown on page 104, a planted wheelbarrow formed a focal point in the design. It is shown here in close-up (Fig. 43). In a tiny front garden that is mostly paved, the whole design may revolve around a display of containers of various kinds (Fig. 44).

Containers should not be overlooked as a way of saying 'welcome' at the front door (Fig. 45). You do not have to use conventional con-

113

Fig. 42   Fig. 43

Fig. 44   Fig. 45

tainers; Fig. 47 shows an unusual use for an old table. The top has been removed and a holder for compost inserted in its place. The result is a cheerful welcome at the door.

Containers of various kinds are, of course, invaluable for brightening up places that would otherwise be uninteresting no matter how well designed the garden otherwise. This terracotta pot of petunias and 'geraniums' (Fig. 46) brightens up what would otherwise be an uninteresting concrete path to the garage. Fig. 48 shows how even everyday plants in a suitable container can be used to provide a focal point in corners of the garden that need a little temporary impact.

Fig. 46

Fig. 47

Fig. 48

Creating a Focal Point

Unless the eye can rest upon some point of interest even the most elaborately designed and constructed garden will lack a sense of purpose and direction. A focal point is an important part of any garden layout. In many gardens you will need more than one focal point; as you turn a corner or enter another part of the garden it always helps to have some feature that arrests attention.

It does not have to be a distant view framed by suitable trees, or a statue, or any of the other obvious contenders. It can be something quite simple like an unusual stone (Fig. 49) that would almost serve as

Fig. 49   *Fig. 50*

a seat. The one in this picture is at the fork of a path away from the main garden, and where you might not expect to find something like this. This is unusual, but it shows that a focal point does not have to be large, tall or expensive.

It could even be a plant if it is spectacular or unusual enough. The picture of a witch and cauldron (Fig. 50) was taken in a small back garden, and because of its originality what would otherwise be a simple yew has become the central attraction of the whole garden.

Wells are quite popular, but how well they work depends on how good and how authentic they look. The one in Fig. 51 looks sufficiently genuine to be effective, and it is given even more impact by the path and very positive framing of it as a focal point. It is worth being cautious with this kind of centrepiece; it can easily go wrong and look contrived and silly.

A garden ornament of some kind is a fairly safe bet on an area of lawn that needs an extra 'something' to transform the scene. A bird-bath or a sundial often provide the answer. They are sensible things that are unlikely to look out of place, and it is usually possible to find one that would be in keeping with the scale of the garden. On the other hand, if you want a real talking point as well as a focal point, and you can afford an impressive (and possibly expensive) sculpture or other ornament then you should be able to achieve an effect like the one in Fig. 52.

If you have a really large garden you can make the focal point dominate the garden. Fig. 53 shows a fine example at Furzey Gardens, at Minstead in Hampshire, England.

116

Fig. 51

Fig. 52

Fig. 53

Somewhere to Sit

A garden should be a place of pleasure as well as work, and with luck you should have time to sit and enjoy your efforts. Most well-designed gardens acknowledge this, and you will nearly always find at least one strategically placed seat in show gardens. There is no reason why you should not follow the same principle and design a garden seat into the overall plan for the garden.

If you have a suitable old tree around which you can build a tree

117

seat, so much the better (Fig. 54). This really does make a super garden feature, and makes good use of the ground beneath and around the tree. Generally seats are best kept away from trees, but this is a rule that can be ignored when it contributes so much to the garden scene. To make the most of a tree seat, paint it white, so that it becomes a positive feature, standing out conspicuously instead of being lost as an unpainted seat would be. It is also a good idea to have something to prevent feet scuffing the ground too much and causing bald patches in the grass. In this case an arrangement of bricks overcomes the problem admirably.

Because you are unlikely to sit on a garden seat for very long at a time, they do not have to be particularly comfortable (you can always use a cushion anyway). Do not be afraid to use stone if this lends the right atmosphere to the garden. Figs. 55 and 56 show how effective even an unpromising seat can be.

The two upright conifers have managed to make one of them into a focal point, helping to offset an otherwise distracting background of open countryside, channelling the eye to a point within the garden, and *then* beyond.

In a small walled garden, the seat can often be usefully placed at an angle across one corner. This helps to take some of the squareness off the view, and it is a useful position from which to appreciate the rest of the garden. In Fig. 57 old wooden railway sleepers have been used to create a series of shallow steps, between which low-growing alpines have been planted. It is the small touches like this that can give a garden an air of distinction.

Fig. 54   *Fig. 55*

Not everyone has a garden where a seat can form an integral part of the design, however, and you should not be deterred from using an ordinary garden seat and positioning it in a place that you think would simply give you a relaxing view of the garden. Do not be deterred by the thought that a conventional wooden garden seat will look too much like a seat in a public park. Fig. 58 shows how well one can fit into a modest private garden.

Fig. 56

Fig. 57

Fig. 58

Dealing with a Slope

Gardening on a slope is not all bad. It can make cutting a lawn awkward work at times, and it can involve extra earthworks in construction, but it also offers wonderful opportunities for creating interest. Rock gardens, water cascades and screes all become so much more natural. A change of level always adds interest to a garden, too.

Even so, a slope can present problems, and you will need to think carefully about the way you deal with slopes in your garden. They do not always occur in the right place, and sometimes it is difficult to decide how best to use the rise or fall in the ground to best advantage. The pictures on these two pages show how some other gardeners have dealt with the problem. They may not be the answer to yours, but they may trigger off ideas that will be right.

One of the most sensible approaches is to make some form of terrace (Fig. 59). The designer of this garden has also used the opportunity to provide a seat round the edge. Steps up to the higher level (Fig. 60) are practical but also add interest.

A much steeper slope calls for more drastic earthworks, and you will need to think carefully before embarking on them, but by planting the retaining wall with suitable plants, such as aubrieta, you can create an impressive spectacle.

If the slope is too gentle to bother terracing, or if you just do not like the idea, and sloping flower beds do not appeal, you could try something like the interesting idea shown in Fig. 61. It solves the problem and makes a fascinating feature at the same time.

Fig. 59

Fig. 60

Fig. 61   Fig. 62

There is no reason why you should not let a path follow a contour of the land to add interest. It gives the path another dimension, and provides the garden with an individual touch (Fig. 62). The only trouble with a design like this is the problem of cutting the grass, especially if the slope is steep.

A Small, Rectangular Back Garden

If you have a large garden, or a small one of interesting shape, you have plenty of scope for imaginative design. If your garden is both small and an uninteresting rectangle, then imagination is bound to be taxed. Yet so many gardens fall into this category, particularly those on modern housing estates.

You can adapt many of the schemes and ideas already outlined in this book, but it is useful to see how two gardeners have successfully overcome the problem of the 'box-shaped' garden. In each case the aim has been to overcome the hard straight edges of the 'box' and to soften the outline with plants.

Fig. 63 shows how a formal outline of paths and the traditional lawn has been given that extra character by adding a 'kink' along the side and angling the corners. Had the width of the bed been too narrow it

121

would have looked mean, and the planting would not have been substantial enough to make an impact. By choosing a few bold (and mainly evergreen) shrubs the garden has impact and the fence acts as a backcloth rather than dominating the scene.

The other garden (Fig. 64) shows a much more informal approach, where the plants themselves hold most of the interest. This is very much a plant-lover's small garden, with plants of contrasting and interesting shape and form being crammed into quite a small space. Most gardens of this size and shape have a rectangular lawn, yet this one has deliberately been made irregular, in fact it is almost circular.

The netting fixed to the wooden fencing is a support for clematis, which were not in flower when this picture was taken. It does, however, show another original approach to making the best of the fencing that is almost invariably a part of the small modern garden.

Fig. 63

Fig. 64

Softening Edges

Hard edges are perfectly acceptable in a formal garden, or perhaps in a patio based on regularly-shaped paving. Among plants, however, harsh straight lines can look ugly and out of sympathy. Sometimes they cannot be avoided, but you can do much to soften them by careful planting. The illustrations on these pages show some of the ways in which plants can be used to break up the harshness of paths and drives.

Often you have little choice but to have a fairly regularly-shaped edge for the drive; it has to be practical. The gravel drive in Fig. 65, however, shows how it can made into a quite attractive feature, with the gravel actually setting off the cascading, low-growing plants planted alongside.

If you do not have a hedge or wall because you either want or have to have an open-plan front garden, the point where garden ends and pavement begins can be a particular problem. Again a wise choice of plants can help. Try to choose low-growing plants with a spreading or trailing habit. If they are colourful in flower, so much the better.

A crazy-paving path tends to be more pleasing anyway, and the lines much less harsh. Even so it will be improved greatly if the plants can be allowed to tumble over it in places (Fig. 66).

If you can attempt to make the path informal and irregular and plant close to the edges, you are fairly sure to have something that will grace your garden.

Fig. 65

Fig. 66

123

A Sawn Log Path

Sawn logs make excellent 'stepping stones' that are very much in sympathy with a garden setting. They can be surprisingly durable, and although they can be quite expensive to buy you must remember that concrete paving slabs can also become costly, and will lack that individual look of logs. You may find a ready supply of logs locally, in which case it is well worth trying to find a way of incorporating them into the garden.

They can look particularly effective meandering purposefully through the garden, perhaps over an area of cultivated soil rather than a lawn (Fig. 67). If you want to make the path more serviceable for wheelbarrows, or simply to make the going easier if you do not want to do a balancing act between logs but like the look of them, try a 'combination' path. Sawn logs can look quite effective bedded into gravel, but try to make them flush with the surface for safety and for visual effect (Fig. 68).

If you have just a few logs, or you simply do not have the size of garden that will enable you to use them to form a large path, try creating a small stepping-stone path across a flower bed, or connecting two parts of the garden across a fairly narrow bed. In fact you do not really need even that excuse, as Fig. 69 shows. Here the logs have been used effectively to create a diversion in a small garden by breaking up a fairly narrow border with a false path. In this case the deception is obvious, but if you make the path disappear behind something, say a bush, then the illusion will be more complete.

Fig. 67

Fig. 68

A Raised Rock Bed

One of the problems with a small modern back garden is the difficulty of adding height. Small gardens are usually flat gardens, and it is always a problem trying to create a sense of interest, and somewhere unseen when all the boundaries are so close.

In Fig. 70, a bold solution has been found by constructing a substantial raised rock bed in one corner of a small rectangular plot. It creates a focal point, at the same time managing to provide an unseen part of the garden that you have to walk round to explore. This is something difficult to achieve in such a small garden, where it is usually possible to take in the whole scene at a single glance.

In this case the compost bin has been placed in the corner of the garden screened by the rock bed, and in a small garden somewhere to put the compost heap is much more of a problem than it is in a larger garden.

Be warned, however, that although a raised bed has paid dividends in this case, it could easily go wrong. You cannot be half-hearted about a feature like this, or it will look silly or pretentious and fail to achieve the desired effect.

Fig. 69

Fig. 70

Index

Figures in italics refer to page numbers of illustrations.